EIGIL KIAER

GARDEN SHRUBS AND TREES

IN COLOUR

Illustrated by
VERNER HANCKE

BLANDFORD PRESS

LONDON

First published in the English edition 1959
English text © 1959 Blandford Press Ltd.,
167 High Holborn London WC1V 6PH
Second impression 1960
Third impression 1963
Fourth impression 1965
Fifth impression 1967
Sixth impression 1969
Revised edition 1973
ISBN 0 7137 0649 X

Based on the Danish edition
Havens buske og Traeer
published by Politikens Forlag 1955

Printed in Holland by The Ysel Press Ltd Deventer
and bound in Great Britain.

PREFACE

Garden Shrubs and Trees is for practical reasons divided into three sections. The first group of illustrations represents the best known and most attractive shrubs and trees for large and small gardens, and includes a selection of the most beautiful roses. Next follow illustrations of the most attractive and widely grown climbers, and finally a large selection of the most characteristic conifers. In each section the plants are arranged alphabetically according to their Latin names, and these are placed before the English names.

Since many gardens very often contain both too many and also the most vigorously-growing shrubs and trees, it is very important for a book of this kind to use some simple and practical means of showing how large any bush or tree will become under normal conditions in the course of twenty or thirty years. Therefore, at the bottom of every plate a small sketch of each plant is included, showing its shape and approximate height and breadth in proportion to a man or an average-sized house. This should be more helpful than mere measurement of height and breadth. But it must be borne in mind that bushes and trees may become even larger when they reach an age of fifty to a hundred years. Maximum heights are therefore given in the text at the back of the book. Shrubs and trees have a lengthy period of life, and one is reluctant to do away with them when they have attained large and magnificent proportions. With this fact in mind it is important to choose these which will grow well together, and will not need to be continually cut back, a process which may also prevent their blossoming.

Trees should be chosen with the greatest care. A beautiful tree not merely adds to the garden where it is growing, but can do a great deal for its neighbourhood, especially in the country, where it can give the whole landscape character and beauty. Several generations may have pleasure from one tree, and it is hoped that this book will help garden growers to choose the right and most satisfactory trees and bushes for their gardens.

The choice of plants has been carried out in collaboration with Mr. R. Lowenmo of Sweden, and all the plates were drawn from life by Verner Hancke. The text has been revised and adapted for British readers by E. B. Anderson.

CONTENTS

1. *Acer campestre,* Field Maple   1a. Seed

2. *Acer negundo variegatum,* Variegated Box Elder   2a. Seed

3. *Acer platanoides,* Norway Maple   3a. Seed

4. *Acer palmatum,* Japanese Maple

5. *Aesculus hippocastanum*, Common Horse Chestnut   5a. Nut

6. *Aesculus carnea*, Red Horse Chestnut

7. *Alnus glutinosa*, Common Alder

8. *Aucuba japonica viridis*

9. *Aucuba japonica variegata*, Gold Dust Tree

10. *Amelanchier laevis*, June Berry

11. *Aralia elata*, Japanese Angelica Tree

12. *Berberis verruculosa,* Warted Barberry
13. *Berberis thunbergii,* Thunberg's Barberry
14. *Berberis thunbergii atropurpurea,* Thunberg's Purple Barberry
15. *Berberis aggregata,* Clustered Barberry
16. *Berberis candidula,* Whitish Barberry
17. *Berberis vulgaris,* Common Barberry

18. *Betula pendula tristis*, Silver Birch

19. *Betula pendula youngii*, Young's Weeping Birch

20. *Buddleia davidii*, Butterfly Bush
21. *Buxus sempervirens arborescens*, Common Box
22. *Buxus sempervirens rotundifolia*, Round Leaved Box

23. *Calluna vulgaris* H.E. Beale, Heather, Ling

24. *Calycanthus floridus,* Carolina Allspice

25. *Callicarpa japonica,* Japanese Violet Berry

26. *Caragana arborescens*, Pea Tree

27. *Carpinus betulus,* Common Hornbeam   27a. Seeds   27b. Catkin

28. *Castanea sativa*, Sweet or Spanish Chestnut   28a. Nut
29. *Catalpa bignonioides*, Indian Bean Tree   29a. Blossom

14

30. *Ceanothus delilianus*, Californian Lilac
31. *Cercidiphyllum japonicum*, Katsura Tree

32. *Chaenomeles speciosa*, Ornamental Quince
33. *Chaenomeles japonica*, Ornamental Quince 33a. Fruit
34. *Cydonia oblonga*, Common Quince

35. *Cladrastis lutea,* Yellow Wood
36. *Colutea arborescens,* Bladder Senna

37. *Cornus mas*, Cornelian Cherry   37a. Fruit   37b. Fruit
38. *Cornus alba sibirica*, Westonbirt Dogwood
39. *Cornus alba spaethii*, Dogwood

40. *Corylopsis willmottiae*, False Hazel
41. *Corylus avellana contorta*, Corkscrew Hazel
42. *Cotinus coggygria*, Smoke Bush
43. *Corylus maxima purpurea*, Purple Filbert

44. *Cotoneaster bullatus*
45. *Cotoneaster dielsianus*
46. *Cotoneaster horizontalis*

47. *Cotoneaster multiflorus*
48. *Cotoneaster salicifolius flocossus*
49. *Cotoneaster adpressus praecox*
49a. Branch with berries

50. *Crataegus orientalis*, Oriental Thorn

51. *Crataegus oxyacantha punicea*, Scarlet Hawthorn   51a. Thorn Hedge

52. *Crataegus oxyacantha* Paul's Scarlet   52a. Haws

53. *Crataegus crus-galli*, Cockspur Thorn

54. *Cytisus praecox,* Warminster Broom
55. *Cytisus purpureus,* Purple Broom
56. *Cytisus kewensis,* Kew Broom
57. *Cytisus scoparius,* Common Broom

58. *Daphne mezereum*, Mezereon   58a. Berries
59. *Davidia involucrata*, Handkerchief Tree

60. *Deutzia rosea*
61. *Deutzia hybrida*

MIRROR PLANT

DEUTZIAS

THESE are among the most delicately beautiful of all the early summer shrubs and because of their size they're excellent for small gardens. Perfectly hardy, they carry masses of pink, purple or white flowers.

There are some superb hybrids, which are usually sold under the name of *Deutzia x hybrida*. With its deep rose flowers, which have a white throat, *D. x kalmiiflora* is particularly suited to small gardens. If you want a large plant the white flowered *D. scabra* fits the bill, reaching a height of 10 ft. Another with pure white flowers, but quite a dwarf at 4 ft, is *D. gracilis* and only a little larger is *D. x elegantissima*, which bears lovely pink to rose fragrant blooms.

Plant from October to February in well-drained soil, preferably in full sunlight or dappled shade.

Cuttings of partly ripe wood should be taken in July and August, and struck in a cold frame.

...y smiles of the lads ...ed from a Majorcan jail ...er being held without ...al for 14 days following ...argument in which a ...bbie died of a heart at-...ck. How cruel of Mrs ...atcher to have said "let ...em rot."

Surely our Prime Minis-: should have stood up for ese five young Britons or least kept her mouth shut until she knew the facts? — M. Townend, Atherton, Lancs.

☐ TORY MPs who jeered calls for Parliament to support world-wide demands for the release of Nelson Mandela on his 70th birthday are sick people.

You don't have to share Mr Mandela's politics to agree that the South African re-gime is barbaric to keep him behind bars for 26 years for oppos-ing the evil of apart-... Mrs C. Jones

62. *Enkianthus campanulatus*, Bell Bush
63. *Elaeagnus commutata*, Silver Berry

26

64. *Euonymus europaeus*, Spindle Tree
65. *Erica vagans*, Cornish Heath
66. *Erica carnea (herbacea)*, Alpine Heath
67. *Euonymus fortunei vegetus*
68. *Euonymus fortunei radicans*

69. *Fagus sylvatica,* Common Beech   69a. Weeping Beech
70. *Fagus sylvatica purpurea,* Purple Beech
71. *Fagus sylvatica laciniata,* Cut Leaved Beech

72. *Ficus carica*, Common Fig Tree
73. *Forsythia intermedia*, Golden Bell   73a. Flowering Branch

74

74a

74b

74c

74

74. *Fraxinus excelsior,* Common Ash

74a. Blossom   74b. Seeds, keys   74c. Shoot

75. *Fuchsia riccartonii*

76. *Genista tinctoria*, Dyer's Greenweed

77. *Ginkgo biloba*, Maidenhair Tree
78. *Gleditsia triacanthos*, Honey Locust

79. *Halesia carolina,* Snowdrop Tree
80. *Hamamelis japonica,* Japanese Witch Hazel
80a. Flowering Branch

81. *Helianthemum nummularium* Lawreson's Pink, Sun Rose

81a. Flower

82. *Helianthemum nummularium* Golden Queen, Sun Rose

83. *Hibiscus syriacus,* Shrubby Mallow

84. *Hippophae rhamnoides*, Sea Buckthorn
85. *Holodiscus discolor*

86. *Hydrangea arborescens*, Tree Hydrangea
87. *Hydrangea macrophylla*, Hortensia Hydrangea
88. *Hydrangea paniculata*, Plumed Hydrangea

89. *Hypericum calycinum*, Rose of Sharon

90. *Hypericum patulum henryi*

91. *Ilex pernyi*, Perny's Holly
92. *Indigofera gerardiana*, Shrubby Indigo
93. *Ilex aquifolium*, Common Holly

94. *Juglans regia*, Walnut   94a. Walnut

95. *Kerria japonica pleniflora*
96. *Kalmia latifolia*, Calico Bush   96a. Blossom

97. *Kolkwitzia amabilis*, Beauty Bush
98. *Laburnocytisus adamii*

99. *Lavandula spica,* Lavender
100. *Laburnum anagyroides,* Golden Rain
100a. Seeds

101. *Ligustrum vulgare*, Common Privet
102. *Ligustrum ovalifolium*, Oval-leaved Privet
103. *Ligustrum vulgare sempervirens*

104. *Liriodendron tulipifera*, Tulip Tree

104a. Seeds   104b. Flower

105. *Lonicera maackii podocarpa,* Shrubby Honeysuckle
105a. Shoot with Berries
106. *Lonicera pileata,* Box Honeysuckle   106a. Berries
107. *Lonicera nitida,* Chinese Honeysuckle

108. *Lonicera syringantha*, Shrubby Honeysuckle
109. *Lonicera tatarica*, Tartarian Honeysuckle

110. *Lycium barbarum,* Box Thorn

111. *Magnolia obovata*

112. *Magnolia sieboldii*
113. *Magnolia soulangiana*
114. *Magnolia stellata*, Star Flowered Magnolia

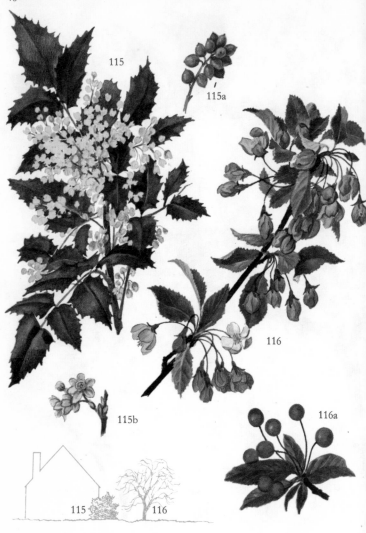

115. *Mahonia aquifolium*, Oregon Grape 115a. Berries 115b. Flower
116. *Malus floribunda*, Flowering Crab 116a. Fruit

117. *Malus* John Downie, Crab Apple   117a. Fruit
118. *Malus halliana,* Flowering Crab

119. *Malus eleyi*, Flowering Crab   119a. Fruit
120. *Malus scheideckeri*, Flowering Crab   120a. Fruit

121. *Mespilus germanica*, Medlar
122. *Morus nigra*, Black Mulberry

123. *Pernettya mucronata*
124. *Paeonia suffruticosa,* Tree Peony

125. *Pieris japonica*   125a. Flower Cluster
126. *Philadelphus coronarius*, Mock Orange
127. *Philadelphus hybrid*, Mock Orange

128a

128b

128

128

128. *Platanus hispanica,* London Plane   128a. Bark   128b. Fruit Ball

129. *Populus alba*, White Poplar   129a. Catkin

130. *Populus canescens*, Grey Poplar

131. *Populus berolinensis*, Berlin Poplar

132. *Populus lasiocarpa*, Red-veined Poplar
133. *Populus nigra italica*, Lombardy Poplar
134. *Populus tremula*, Aspen
134a. and 134b.   Catkins

135. *Potentilla fruticosa*, Shrubby Cinquefoil
136. *Potentilla fruticosa farreri*, Shrubby Cinquefoil
137. *Potentilla fruticosa veitchii*, Shrubby Cinquefoil

138. *Prunus dulcis*, Almond

139. *Prunus avium plena*, Double Gean

140. *Prunus cerasifera pissardii*, Purple Leaved Plum

141. *Prunus laurocerasus,* Cherry Laurel

142. *Prunus padus,* Bird Cherry

143. *Prunus spinosa,* Sloe   143a. Fruit, Sloe

144. *Prunus tenella,* Dwarf Russian Almond

60

145. *Prunus* Amanogawa, Japanese Cherry
146. *Prunus* Hisakura, Japanese Cherry
147. *Prunus* Shirotae (Mount Fuji), Japanese Cherry

148. *Prunus subhirtella,* Spring Cherry
149. *Prunus triloba,* Flowering Almond

150. *Pterocarya fraxinifolia*, Wing Nut
151. *Ptelea trifoliata*, Hop Tree

152. *Pyracantha coccinea*, Firethorn 152a. Branch with Berries

153. *Quercus rubra*, Red Oak   153a. Autumn Colour
154. *Quercus robur*, English Oak   154a. Acorn

155. *Rhamnus frangula*, Alder Buckthorn

156. *Rhododendron catawbiense*

157. *Rhododendron* Parson's Gloriosum
158. *Rhododendron* Caractacus
159. *Rhododendron* Pink Pearl

160. *Rhododendron* Rosamundii
161. *Rhododendron ferrugineum*, Alpen Rose
162. *Rhododendron* Princess Marika

163. *Rhododendron*, Mollis Azalea type
164. *Rhododendron*, Ghent Azalea type
165. *Rhododendron praecox*
166. *Rhododendron schlippenbachii*

167. *Rhus typhina laciniata*, Cut-leaved Stag's Horn Sumach
168. *Rhus typhina*, Stag's Horn Sumach   168a. Seeds

169. *Ribes sanguineum*, Flowering Currant   169a. Deep red form
170. *Ribes alpinum*, Alpine Currant   170a. Hedge
171. *Ribes odoratum*, Buffalo Currant

172. *Robinia pseudoacacia decaisneana*, False Acacia

173. *Rosa canina,* Dog Rose
174. *Rosa carolina,* Carolina Rose
175. *Rosa heleniae,* Helen Wilson's Rose
176. *Rosa foetida,* Austrian Briar
177. *Rosa moyesii,* Shrub Rose   177a. Heps

178. *Rosa hugonis*, Shrub Rose
179. *Rosa omeiensis pteracantha*, Red Thorn Mt Omei Rose
180. *Rosa omeiensis*, Mt Omei Rose

181. *Rosa rugosa,* Ramanas Rose
181a. Heps
181b. White variety
182. *Rosa rubiginosa* Lady Penzance, Sweet Briar

183. *Rosa spinosissima* variety, Scotch or Burnet Rose
184. *Rosa blanda,* Smooth or Meadow Rose   184a. Heps

185. *Rosa centifolia muscosa,* Moss Rose
186. *Rosa borboniana,* Bourbon Rose

187. Hybrid Perpetual Rose General Jacqueminot
188. Hybrid Perpetual Rose Mrs. John Laing
189. Hybrid Perpetual Rose Frau Karl Druschki
190. Hybrid Perpetual Rose Charles Bonnet

191. Hybrid Tea Rose Geheimrat Duisberg
192. Hybrid Tea Rose New Yorker

193. Hybrid Tea Rose Betty Uprichard
194. Hybrid Tea Rose Dainty Bess
195. Hybrid Tea Rose Dame Edith Helen
196. Hybrid Tea Rose Edina
197. Hybrid Tea Rose Eclipse

198. Hybrid Tea Rose Peace
199. Hybrid Tea Rose Picture
200. Hybrid Tea Rose Spek's Yellow
201. Hybrid Tea Rose Talisman

202. Hybrid Tea Rose Ena Harkness
203. Hybrid Tea Rose Etoile de Hollande
204. Hybrid Tea Rose Edith Nelly Perkins
205. Hybrid Tea Rose Elite

206. Hybrid Tea Rose Flaming Sunset
207. Hybrid Tea Rose Mme. Caroline Testout
208. Hybrid Tea Rose Mrs. Pierre S. Dupont
209. Hybrid Tea Rose Ophelia

210. Floribunda Rose Alain
211. Floribunda Rose Frensham
212. Polyantha Pompon Rose Ellen Poulsen
213. Floribunda Rose Julie Poulsen
214. Floribunda Rose Fashion

215. Floribunda Rose Goldilocks
216. Floribunda Rose Gruss an Aachen
217. Floribunda Rose Irene of Denmark
218. Floribunda Rose Karen Poulsen

219. Floribunda Rose Margot Koster
220. Floribunda Rose Dick Koster
221. Floribunda Rose Orange Triumph
222. Floribunda Rose Danish Gold
223. Floribunda Rose Poulsen's Pink
224. Floribunda Rose Red Hat

225. Rambler Rose American Pillar
226. Rambler Rose Dorothy Perkins
227. Rambler Rose Paul's Scarlet Climber
228. Rambler Rose Easlea's Golden Rambler

229. Rambler Rose Excelsa

230. Large-flowered Climbing Rose Gloire de Dijon

231. Rambler Rose Dr. W. Van Fleet

232. *Salix chrysocoma*, Weeping Willow
233. *Salix acutifolia*, Violet Willow
234. *Salix viminalis*, Common Osier
235. *Salix caprea*, Goat Willow or Great Sallow

236. *Sambucus nigra*, Common Elder
237. *Sambucus racemosa*, Red Berried Elder
238. *Sambucus canadensis*, American Elderberry

239. *Sorbaria arborea glabrata*, Tree Spiraea
240. *Arundinaria nitida*, Bamboo

241. *Sorbus aucuparia*, Mountain Ash or Rowan
242. *Sorbus intermedia*, Swedish Whitebeam

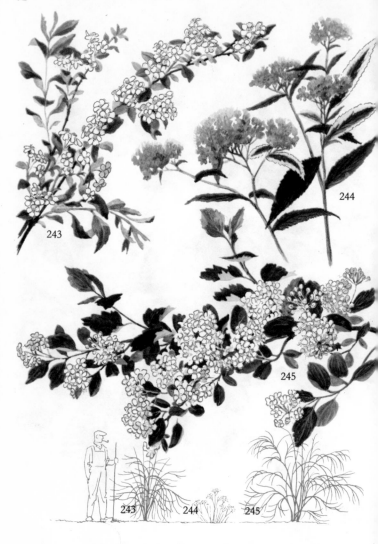

243. *Spiraea arguta,* Bridal Wreath, Foam of May
244. *Spiraea bumalda* Anthony Waterer
245. *Spiraea vanhouttei*

246. *Stephanandra incisa*
247. *Symphoricarpos rivularis,* Snowberry
248. *Symphoricarpos chenaultii,* Hybrid Coral Berry   248a. Berries

249. *Syringa chinensis,* Rouen Lilac

250. *Syringa reflexa,* Nodding Lilac

251. *Syringa tomentella,* Downy Lilac

252. *Syringa vulgaris* Souvenir de Louis Spaeth, Lilac
253. *Syringa vulgaris* Madame Lemoine, Lilac
254. *Syringa vulgaris* Michel Buchner, Lilac

255. *Tamarix pentandra,* Tamarisk   255a. Spray of Blossom

256. *Tilia platyphyllos*, Broad-leaved Lime

257. *Ulmus glabra*, Wych or Scotch Elm

257a. Flower   257b. Seeds

258. *Viburnum carlesii*

259. *Viburnum farreri (fragrans)*

260. *Viburnum lantana*, Wayfaring Tree

260a. Berries

261. *Viburnum opulus sterile*, Snowball Tree
262. *Viburnum rhytidophyllum*
263. *Viscum album*, Mistletoe

264. *Vinca major*, Greater Periwinkle
265. *Vince minor*, Lesser Periwinkle
266. *Vinca major variegata*, Variegated Greater Periwinkle

267. *Weigela* Abel Carriere
268. *Weigela* Mont Blanc
269. *Weigela* Le Printemps
270. *Weigela* Styriaca

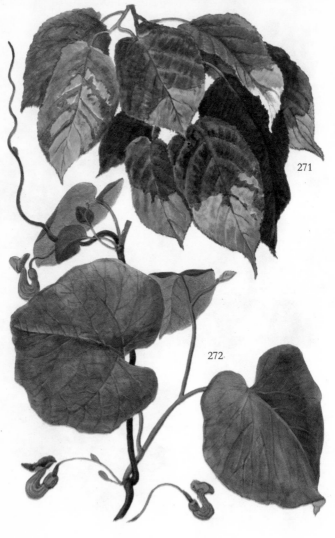

271. *Actinidia kolomikta*
272. *Aristolochia macrophylla,* Dutchman's Pipe

273. *Celastrus scandens*, Staff Tree

274. *Campsis radicans*, Trumpet Vine

275. *Clematis montana rubens*, Mountain Clematis

276. *Clematis* Comtesse de Bouchaud
277. *Clematis jackmanii*
278. *Clematis* The President
279. *Clematis* Lasurstern
280. *Clematis* Nelly Moser

281. *Clematis tangutica*, Mongolian Clematis   281a. Seed Head
282. *Clematis vitalba*, Travellers Joy
283. *Clematis viticella kermesina*

284. *Hedera helix*, Common Ivy

285. *Hedera helix arborescens*, Tree Ivy

286. *Hedera helix hibernica*, Irish Ivy

287. *Hedera colchica*, Persian Ivy

288. *Hydrangea petiolaris*, Climbing Hydrangea
289. *Jasminum nudiflorum*, Winter Jasmine
289a. Flowering Branch

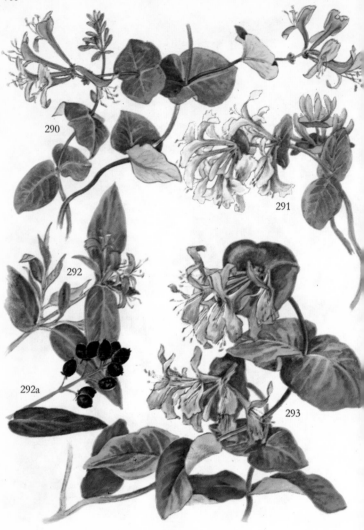

290. *Lonicera beckrotii*, Honeysuckle
291. *Lonicera caprifolium*, Perfoliate Honeysuckle
292. *Lonicera henryi*, Honeysuckle   292a. Berries
293. *Lonicera tellmanniana*, Honeysuckle

294. *Parthenocissus tricuspidata*, Boston Ivy
295. *Parthenocissus quinquefolia*, Virginia Creeper

296. *Polygonum baldschuanicum,* Russian Vine
297. *Wisteria sinensis,* Chinese Wisteria

298. *Vitis vinifera,* Grape Vine
299. *Vitis vinifera* Precose de Malingre, Grape Vine
300. *Vitis vinifera* Burgundy Blue, Grape Vine

301. *Abies concolor*, Colorado White Fir   301a. Cone
302. *Abies homolepis*, Nikko Fir
303. *Abies cephalonica*, Grecian Fir

304
304a
304b
305
306
304 304 305 306

304. *Abies procera glauca*, Blue Noble Fir
304a. Cones   304b. Cone Scale
305. *Abies pinsapo*, Spanish Fir
306. *Abies alba*, European Silver Fir

307. *Cedrus deodara,* Deodar
308. *Cedrus atlantica glauca,* Blue Cedar

309. *Chamaecyparis lawsoniana,* Lawson Cypress
310. *Chamaecyparis lawsoniana allumii,* Lawson Cypress
311. *Chamaecyparis lawsoniana wisselii,* Lawson Cypress

312. *Chamaecyparis nootkatensis*, Nootka Cypress
313. *Chamaecyparis nootkatensis pendula*, Weeping Nootka Cypress

314. *Chamaecyparis obtusa*, Hinoki Cypress
315. *Chamaecyparis obtusa nana*, Dwarf Hinoki Cypress

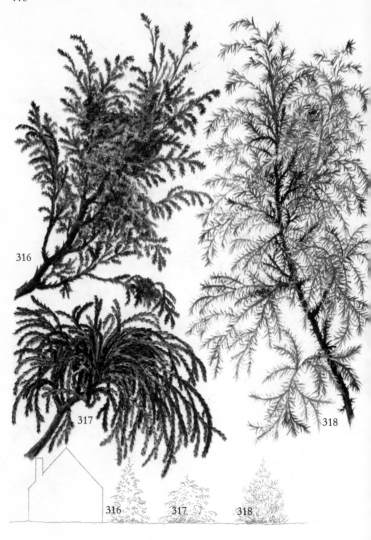

316. *Chamaecyparis pisifera plumosa,* Sawara Cypress
317. *Chamaecyparis pisifera filifera,* Slender Sawara Cypress
318. *Chamaecyparis pisifera squarrosa,* Sawara Cypress

319. *Cryptomeria japonica lobbii*, Lobb's Japanese Cedar
320. *Cryptomeria japonica elegans*, Japanese Cedar

321. *Juniperus media pfitzeriana,* Pfitzer Juniper
322. *Juniperus chinensis pyramidalis,* Chinese Juniper
323. *Juniperus communis suecica,* Swedish Juniper   323a. Fruit
324. *Juniperus horizontalis,* Creeping Juniper

325. *Juniperus chinensis japonicà,* Dwarf Chinese Juniper

326. *Juniperus sabina tamariscifolia,* Tamarisk Savin

327. *Juniperus squamata meyeri,* Meyer's Juniper

328. *Juniperus virginiana glauca,* Pencil Juniper

329. *Larix decidua*, Common Larch
329a. Branch with Cones
330. *Larix kaempferi (leptolepis)*, Japanese Larch

331. *Picea glauca,* White Spruce   331a. Cone
332. *Picea abies,* Norway Spruce, Christmas Tree   332a. Cone
333. *Picea glauca conica,* Dwarf White Spruce

334. *Picea pungens glauca*, Blue Spruce
335. *Picea omorica*, Serbian Spruce   335a. Cone
336. *Picea sitchensis*, Sitka Spruce   336a. Cone

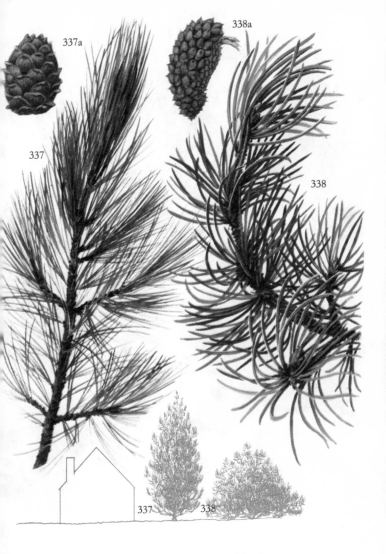

337. *Pinus cembra,* Arolla Pine   337a. Cone
338. *Pinus contorta,* Beach Pine   338a. Cone

339. *Pinus mugo*, Mountain Pine
340. *Pinus nigra*, Austrian Pine   340a. Cone
341. *Pinus parviflora*, Japanese White Pine

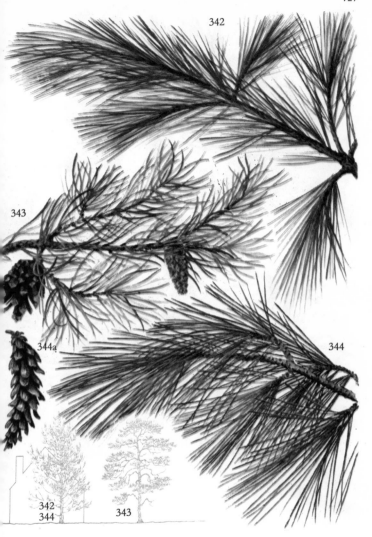

342. *Pinus peuce*, Macedonian Pine
343. *Pinus silvestris*, Scots Pine
344. *Pinus strobus*, Weymouth Pine   344a. Cone

345. *Pseudotsuga menziesii*, Oregon Douglas Fir   345a. Cone
346. *Sciadopitys verticillata*, Umbrella Pine

347. *Sequoiadendron giganteum*, Wellingtonia
348. *Taxodium distichum*, Swamp Cypress

349. *Taxus baccata*, Common or English Yew   349a. Yew Hedges

350. *Taxus baccata fastigiata*, Irish Yew

351. *Taxus baccata aurea*, Golden Yew

352. *Thuja occidentalis,* American Arbor-vitae   352a. Thuya Hedges
353. *Thuja plicata,* Western Red Cedar
354. *Thuja standishii,* Japanese Arbor-vitae

355
357
356

355
357
356

355. *Thujopsis dolabrata*, Hiba
356. *Tsuga heterophylla*, Western Hemlock
357. *Tsuga canadensis*, Eastern Hemlock

DESCRIPTIONS OF PLANTS

In the descriptions below, the numbers correspond to the numbers used in the plates. Height, width, and time of blossoming, may vary according to local soil conditions and climate.

I BROAD-LEAFED SHRUBS AND TREES

All the shrubs and trees illustrated up to page 101 are broad-leafed plants with normal flowers and dicotyledonous seedlings. Some of them are deciduous, some semi-evergreen, some evergreen, as stated in the text.

1 Acer campestre
Field Maple

Habitat: Europe, Western Asia. When young, a broad, compact bush, and when older, a little tree with a broad, close, round crown, and knotted branches. It tolerates shade well and is an easily grown plant, which prefers a light, moist, chalky soil.

It makes a very good hedge, and turns an attractive yellow hue in the autumn. Height may be from 35 to 45 ft.

2 Acer negundo variegatum
Variegated Box Elder

Habitat: North America. A small tree of rapid growth, with a light, open habit and pretty, variegated leaves. It shows to best advantage on its own, or with *Acer palmatum* (No. 4) growing beneath it.

It does well in ordinary heavy loam, but should not be exposed to wind. It reaches 25 to 30 ft in height.

3 Acer platanoides
Norway Maple

Habitat: Europe, Asia Minor. A handsome tree which blossoms profusely before the leaves appear; having small yellow flowers in half umbels. Its requirements are few and it is able to stand both shade and wind. It is useful as a sheltering hedge or as a tree standing on its own in a large garden. Height some 50 to 60 ft.

Other attractive varieties of Acer are: *Acer pseudoplatanus,* which grows somewhat larger than *Acer platanoides*, but may be put to similar uses; and *Acer saccharinum*, also tall, but with a more graceful pendant growth. The leaves are most attractive, silver-white on the under-side, and turning a brilliant yellow in the autumn. It does best in a chalky soil, containing plenty of humus. These Acer varieties should be pruned in January only, and not on any account in the spring, when there would be grave risk of much bleeding on account of the strong flow of sap.

4 Acer palmatum
Japanese Maple

Habitat: Korea, Japan. This delightful little maple has some exceedingly beautiful varieties with finely-divided leaves, or leaves shaped like open hands 12-palmate, the colours being yellow, green or red. These varieties may be anything from barely 3 ft to about 10 ft in height, and they have a most picturesque, crooked way of growing, which makes them suitable for large rock-gardens, for standing alone on a lawn, or among carpeting plants like Asarum, Vinca, Stephanandra.

In a dry, sunny position, they will turn a brilliant colour in the autumn. They should have a light soil with plenty of humus, and not be exposed to strong winds.

5 Aesculus hippocastanum
Common Horse Chesthut

Habitat: Asia Minor, the Caucausus. This familiar and lovely tree, with the characteristic large buds and beautiful, upright flower-clusters, is unfortunately suited only to parks and avenues. It is one of the greediest of trees and casts a dense shade; planted in an ordinary garden it may do irreparable harm. On the other hand, when severely pollarded, it loses its fine crown. It attains a height of 80 ft or so.

6 Aesculus carnea
Red Horse Chestnut

Habitat: North America. In many ways resembles the common horse chestnut, but is somewhat broader and not quite so tall. Anybody wanting a tree with red blossoms will be a little disappointed with the rather dirty-red clusters, and would do much better to choose a twice-flowering red thorn instead. Like the common horse chestnut, it is suited only to very spacious surroundings.

7 Alnus glutinosa
Common Alder

Habitat: Siberia, North Africa. One of our most damp-loving trees, which will grow excellently in a marshy situation, provided it is free from chalk. Useful as wind break, or as 'nurse trees' that is to say, quickly-growing trees put in temporarily among others which take a long time to mature.

Alnus glutinosa may be used as a tall sheltering hedge around orchards or gardens in the country. It reaches 60 to 80 ft in height.

Another unexacting and wind-resistant variety of alder is *Alnus incana*, which, however, does not grow so well in a damp position, but thrives in a light, poor soil. It has the same uses as *Alnus glutinosa*. Alders will stand severe pruning.

8 Aucuba japonica viridis

Habitat: Japan. One of the best shade-loving evergreen shrubs which will do excellently in even very shady spots in old gardens or in courtyards. The red berries are attractive, but for these it is necessary to make sure that one has both male and female forms. It seldom exceeds 5 ft.

9 Aucuba japonica variegata
Gold Dust Tree

Although originally introduced as *A. japonica*, this variety should now be known as *A. japonica variegata*.
Habitat: Japan. This bears leaves with yellow spots. The effect alongside some evergreens, especially conifers, can be slightly unpleasing; it should therefore be used only with broad-leafed evergreen bushes, such as *Prunus laurocerasus, Mahonia, Viburnum rhytidophyllum* etc. (See sections on these.)

10 Amelanchier laevis
June Berry

Habitat: North America. One of the most beautiful of all flowering trees which should be grown much more frequently. It blossoms profusely in May, and the young growth bears charming reddish leaves which in the autumn turn a brilliant colour. It thrives in ordinary good soil, preferably in a sunny spot. Height, some 10 to 15 ft.

11 Aralia elata
Japanese Angelica Tree

Habitat: Japan and Korea. A remarkable shrub with long, thick, extremely spiney stems, whose appearance gives it the name The Devil's Walking-Stick. In the summer it has charming, finely-divided leaves of enormous size and in a hot season there appear very large and beautiful, pale-yellow clusters of flowers at the tops of the stems. It should stand alone on a lawn, or between low shrubs. It must have good, rich soil to produce the most beautiful effect. Height about 10 or 12 ft.

12 Berberis verruculosa
Warted Barberry

Habitat: China. A very useful little evergreen shrub with extremely prickly leaves, which will stand a good deal of shade and poor soil. It has charming small flowers in June, and reaches some 5 ft.

13 Berberis thunbergii
Thunberg's Barberry

Habitat: Japan. Probably one of the most commonly-used of the newer bushes for low hedges, as a shrub in the front of larger groups or as a close screen in front gardens facing a public highway. It is very prickly. It has pretty yellow flowers in May, and in dry positions will turn a delightful colour in the autumn, besides bearing attractive red berries. It attains some 5 ft in height, and will stand hard cutting-back annually.

14 Berberis thunbergii atropurpurea
Thunberg's Purple Barberry

Habitat: Japan. A pretty, red-leafed variety of the shrub just described, and equally robust.

15 Berberis aggregata
Clustered Barberry

Habitat: Western China. A compact shrub, whose main attraction is that it bears a profusion of pretty green, later red berries in small clusters like grapes. The berries are edible and rich in vitamins. The shrub is deciduous, reaches about 5 ft in height, and may be grown as a hedge, or standing by itself. *Berberis polyantha* resembles it and is a heavy bearer.

16 Berberis candidula
Whitish Barberry

Habitat: central China. A low, compact evergreen shrub, with prickly leaves. Unexacting, able to stand shade, and hardy. An excellent plant for planting between large evergreens, as an edging beside a lawn, or as a hedge on a low bank facing a public road. Grows about 2 ft high, and has a spreading, flat manner of growth.

A very lovely flowering barberry is *Berberis stenophylla semperflorens*; which bears scented, yellow, hanging clusters of flowers in May or June, and flowers again attractively several times in the course of the summer. It is of a spreading growth with long, fine, arching stems. It is an evergreen, and attains some 5 ft in height.

Other useful barberries are the low-growing *Berberis buxifolia var. nana*, which is evergreen and may be used for the front of borders; and *Berberis polyantha* which is much like *Berberis aggregata*, and bears, as it does, pretty, coral-red berries.

17 Berberis vulgaris
Common Barberry

Habitat: Europe. It is one of the most attractive of hardy shrubs, both for its blossom and masses of coral berries in the autumn, which the birds dislike and so leave alone. At one time there were numerous varieties differing in the colour of the berries — white, yellow and purple.

18 Betula pendula tristis
Silver Birch

Habitat: Europe. A much-loved, familiar and beautiful tree, which takes little nourishment from the soil. It does well both in extremely dry, light soils, and in very damp ones, but it attains its most beautiful condition in good ground with a generous degree of moisture. Strong winds are the worst enemy of the birch; but another is severe pruning, which will destroy the lovely form of its crown. If the crown must be thinned out somewhat, or made symmetrical, this should always be done in the winter, and certainly not in March or April, when the flow of the sap is such that whole branches may bleed to death.

The species varies a good deal: the pendant habit may be slight, or it may be pronounced. Experts can tell when a sapling is still quite small whether it will become a weeping birch or not. The magnificent, weeping crown develops only after some years, however. The birch is best planted as growth commences. It grows to some 65 ft.

Other valuable birch species are: *Betula papyrifera*. Habitat: North America. This birch gets its name from the fact that the trunk has a charming, paper-like, peeling bark, pure white in colour. It is an unexacting tree, and more tolerant of wind than the last species; but it is not quite so weeping in its mode of growth. Its height is about 50 ft. *Betula pubescens*, the most damp-tolerant of all the birches, and therefore well suited for planting along the margins of lakes, or in marshes but not ones on chalk. In other ways it resembles *Betula pendula tristis*.

19 Betula pendula youngii
Young's Weeping Birch

This birch with a most pronounced weeping quality is often grown in churchyards for its sad appearance. But its manner of growth is so abnormal that it does not become a proper tree at all, but a dense shrub, almost like a stork's nest. In gardens the lovely form *Betula pendula* is to be preferred. *Betula pendula fastigiata*, on the other hand, is an upright, attractive tree, which forms a slender compact crown of great beauty.

20 Buddleia davidii
Butterfly Bush

Habitat: China. One of the most lovely of all flowering shrubs. Its long, deep-purple flower-clusters attract all the butterflies. In height and in width it reaches about 12 ft, but it must be pruned moderately each year at the beginning of April. It is most beautiful when it stands by itself in the middle of a lawn. There are many other delightful varieties: for example, 'Royal Red', which is a brilliant reddish purple, 'Hyacinth', which is pure blue, 'Ile de France', dark purple, with very long flower-sprays, and *Buddleia nanhoensis*, with a very slender habit and countless small pale violet sprays.

21 Buxus sempervirens arborescens
Common Box

Habitat: Western Asia, Southern Europe. For many years this excellent, evergreen bush was used as an edging or hedge around flowerbeds. However, its use in the past for making edgings in cemeteries has caused some reluctance to growing it in a private garden. But it would be foolish to reject such a useful plant for this reason. In particular the large-leafed variety, *Buxus sempervirens rotundifolia,* should be used much in gardens where shade and poor air conditions make it difficult to get attractive, compact masses of foliage. Box ought also to be used more where thick hedges are required on terraces or around flower gardens. But the dwarf *Buxus sempervirens suffruticosa*, suitable for borders around beds and so on, will hardly find much use in future, since more suitable plants are now available. Box grows best in a deep soil containing plenty of humus, and the ground around it should never be dug deeply.

22 Buxus sempervirens rotundifolia
Round Leaved Box

Habitat: Western Asia, southern Europe. The most robust and vigorous variety, which is best used along with holly, *Prunus laurocerasus*, *Lonicera nitida*, and other evergreen, broadleafed bushes. Grows to 12 ft in height and width. Otherwise like No. 21.

23 Calluna vulgaris
H. E. Beale, *Heather, Ling*

Habitat: Europe, Asia Minor. This attractive variety of Ling can look very well in a bed prepared with peat or heath-soil along with other acid-soil plants. But the soil must be acid, that is to say, lacking in chalk (pH value 4 to 5), and the plants put in when quite small. This applies also to bell heathers, which should be moved and planted only when small. Flowers in September or October.

Other useful and pretty varieties worthy of mention are: *Calluna vulgaris*, '*Mullion*', low-growing and with profuse blossoms, and *Calluna vulgaris*, '*Goldsworth Crimson*', which reaches about a foot high, and blooms prettily with long purple spikes of flowers.

24 Calycanthus floridus
Carolina Allspice

Habitat: North America. This bush bears very unusual and beautiful flowers which have a faint smell of caramel; although real caramel is not obtained from this plant. It is of spreading growth, attains about 6 ft in height, and needs good soil.

25 Callicarpa japonica
Japanese Violet Berry

Habitat: Japan. A pretty and symmetrical shrub which becomes about 6 ft high and is grown chiefly for its small, brilliant purple fruits, which when the leaves drop make the whole tree a mass of colour. To obtain a good set of berries more than one plant must be grown. It does best in a sheltered spot in good, deep earth, rich in humus.

26 Caragana arborescens
Pea Tree

Habitat: Siberia and Manchuria. One of the least exacting and most hardy bushes, which will grow in the poorest soils and exposed to strong winds. It can be recommended both as a clipped and a free-growing sheltering hedge. It does well even in the most open places near the sea-shore. It is also good as a plant for dry, sun-baked hill-slopes. Its height is 12 ft. It has two varieties: *Caragana arborescens pendula*, which develops into a small, weeping tree of doubtful beauty, and a dwarf type *Caragana arborescens nana*, which has a grotesque, crooked way of growing.

27 Carpinus betulus
Common Hornbeam

Habitat: Europe. Probably best known as a hedge plant, and very well suited for this, as it is compact, easy to clip, and fairly tolerant of shade. It may also be grown as a free-standing tree in dry conditions, when it becomes attractive and symmetrical, and develops a graceful trunk. It reaches 50 ft.

28 Castanea sativa
Sweet or Spanish Chestnut

Habitat: North Africa and Southern Europe. A handsome, massive tree, with a picturesque crown and glossy, dark-green leaves. When it is in bloom, the crown of the tree is full of long yellow catkins, which have a faint smell. Later come the prickly, green fruits, which split when ripe to reveal the familiar shiny, edible nuts. It is only in very warm summers that they reach such a size as to be worth eating. It is grown as a free-standing tree on spacious, sweeping lawns, or as a bush between evergreens; in the latter case, it must be pruned severely every two years. Given the right conditions, it attains a height of 70 ft.

29 Catalpa bignonioides
Indian Bean Tree

Habitat: North America. For a late-flowering, beautiful tree of moderate size, no better choice could be made than Catalpa. It has large, attractive leaves. It requires good soil, rich in humus, and a warm, sheltered position. It does extremely well as an individual tree in a front garden, or on a lawn. Its one disadvantage is that the leaves come very late. It reaches 50 ft or so in height.

30 Ceanothus delilianus
Californian Lilac

A hybrid between *C. americanus* and *C. coeruleus*. A small shrub with slender branches, which should be cut back hard every year. It flowers profusely in August or September on the new season's shoots. It does best in a soil containing some humus and free from chalk, and may be used in company with other slender, low-growing flowering bushes, such as Hypericum and Potentilla, in front of borders. About 3 ft high, either more or less, according to the severity of the pruning.

An excellent variety is 'Gloire de Versailles', which has handsome, dark-blue flowers.

31 Cercidiphyllum japonicum
Katsura Tree

Habitat: China. An attractive tree of light build, which is cultivated for its lovely and delicately-shaped leaves, which are reddish when they first come out, and in the autumn turn a remarkably vivid yellow, pin, or red. It does best in a slightly damp situation, and reaches some 45 ft in height.

32 Chaenomeles speciosa
Ornamental Quince

Habitat: China. A quince bush of very vigorous growth, with thorny stems. It produces a great number of pretty, vivid-red or rose flowers in May; later yellowish-green, lemon-like fruits appear, which are strongly scented. They cannot be eaten raw, but make extremely good jam or jelly or quince cheese. Heavy loam and a sunny position are required. Height, about 6 ft.

33 Chaenomeles japonica
Ornamental Quince

Habitat: Japan. A shrub of low spreading growth, which flowers freely. It grows best in a very dry, sunny spot, and is well-suited for low hedges, and for planting on slopes. It reaches a height of some 5 ft, and a breadth of 6 ft. The fruits turn a brilliant yellow and have a pleasant smell.

34 Cydonia oblonga
Common Quince

Habitat: Central Asia. A lovely little tree with picturesque, bent way of growing. Blossoms attractively in May, and has pretty, lemon-yellow fruits in great numbers in the autumn. The fruits cannot be eaten raw, but will make jam etc. This quince is also used as a stock for other fruit-trees. By this means dwarf trees may be obtained. The height of old trees may be as much as 25 ft, but a more usual height is about 15 ft. There is a type with fruit the shape of an apple and another with the shape of a pear.

35   Cladrastis lutea   *Yellow Wood*

Habitat: North America. A tree with an unusually attractive habit of growth. It has fine, pinnate leaves, and in the middle of the summer it bears sprays, up to 1½ ft long, of scented white pea-flowers, In the autumn the tree turns a delightful, vivid yellow.

Grows up to 50 ft in height, and looks very fine by itself on a lawn in a sunny situation. It requires good average soil.

36   Colutea arborescens
Bladder Senna

Habitat: North Africa. It is most frequently grown on account of its remarkably modest requirement for nourishment, and will thrive in dry, poor soil, though it should be chalky. It bears yellow pea-flowers from June onwards until the end of the summer. The air-filled pods give the bush the name of Bladder-Pod. The seeds are poisonous. Height, some 9 ft.

37   Cornus mas
Cornelian Cherry

Habitat: Southern Europe and Western Asia. In spacious surroundings a very handsome bush that may be grown either at the back of a border or grouped with other free-standing shrubs and trees. It is particularly useful because it blossoms early. Its countless, tiny yellow flowers that are a mass of stamens, are the first sign of approaching spring. Broad and com-

pact of growth, it reaches about 10 ft in height. It may also serve as a hedge, when it may be clipped closely, and even made quite narrow, without losing the ability to blossom. It grows best in good soil with plenty of humus, and will stand a good deal of shade, though this results in fewer flowers.

38   Cornus alba sibirica
Westonbirt Dogwood

Habitat: Siberia. This is grown chiefly on account of its glossy, red stems which look delightful in the winter-time. It is an unexacting plant, and tolerates shade and damp. It has a spreading, slightly pendant mode of growth, which means that it should be planted in the front of large borders. It reaches 10 or 12 ft in height, and should be rejuvenated every few years by the cutting away of old branches.

39   Cornus alba spaethii
Dogwood

Habitat: Siberia. This is somewhat less vigorous of growth than the last plant, and should be placed in a sunny spot so that the variegated leaves may acquire a brilliant colour.

40   Corylopsis willmottiae
False Hazel

Habitat: Western China. Since it would be difficult to have too many early-flowering shrubs, this delightful 12 ft bush is to be recommended. At the beginning of April it produces clusters of catkin-like flowers. A variety with a lighter growth, and less vigorous, is *Corylopsis pauciflora*.

41   Corylus avellana contorta
Corkscrew Hazel

Habitat: Europe. The common hazel is quite familiar, but this variety is a curious plant with a peculiar manner of growth. It can look most amusing when set among dwarf bushes or rock-plants, and with the years may develop the most grotesque shapes. It is very slow-growing and seldom becomes more than 6 ft high.

42 Cotinus coggygria
Smoke Bush

Habitat: Southern Europe and China. This bush should stand alone in a dry, chalky soil, if it is to acquire its most characteristic appearance, that is to say, of it is to become completely covered with flowers appearing like pinkish smoke in the summer; and in the winter with fine silky hairs. It becomes a spreading bush and may be 20 ft wide, while only 10 ft high.

The variety *Cotinus coggygria purpureus* has delightful reddish leaves, and a beautiful colouration in the autumn.

43 Corylus maxima purpurea
Purple Filbert

Habitat: Europe and Western Asia. An attractive bush with deep-purple leaves which grows best in the shelter of larger trees and bushes, and in a light, damp soil containing plenty of humus. It reaches some 18 ft in height.

44 Cotoneaster bullatus

Habitat: Western China. The coton-easter family offers some of the most valuable of all shrubs among its many species. There are some low-growing types, like *Cotoneaster dammeri*, which lies flat on the ground, or on rocks, and tall varieties like the one named above, which is extremely vigorous and may reach 12 ft or so in height. This one is well suited to stand alone on a lawn, or between low bushes, or to form part of a large group. It does well in all soils, but develops most charmingly in the full sun, and requires good light if it is to bear its red fruits in large numbers.

45 Cotoneaster dielsianus

Habitat: China. One of the most beautiful and graceful of the coton-easter species. It bears fruits very freely which hang in clusters among the frail twigs. Reaches 6 to 9 ft in height and does not require pruning; merely a little thinning and shaping now and then.

46 Cotoneaster horizontalis

Habitat: Western China. Its low, spreading growth makes it very suitable for planting on slopes or along the side of a house, and also in the foreground of borders. The pretty, red berries develop best in open, sunny spots. Grows some 3 ft in height.

47 Cotoneaster multiflorus

Habitat: Western China. Very profusely flowering (May to June), but is white flowers have an unpleasant smell. It bears many red berries and has a light, graceful growth. Height, 6 to 9 ft.

48 Cotoneaster salicifolius floccosus

An evergreen cotoneaster with attac-tive, long, hanging branches, shiny, dark-green and delightful, reddish-orange berries in clusters. *Cotoneaster salicifolius floccosus* greatly resembles the above, and like it may be used among broad-leafed evergreen bushes. Reaches about 10 ft in height and the same breadth.

49 Cotoneaster adpressus praecox

Habitat: Western China. Its low, sprawling growth makes it most useful for planting on slopes, or around crazy-paving. It bears pretty rose-coloured flowers in June, and large orange berries in the late summer.

50 Crataegus orientalis
Oriental Thorn

The thorns are some of our most

easily satisfied and also most wind-resistant trees. They may be used either as part of a wind-break, as tall, unclipped sheltering hedges, or as finely-clipped hedges between gardens. They are also attractive as single trees on a lawn, and may be grown in smaller gardens on account of their modest size, pretty blossoms, and delightful fruits, which remain on the tree far into the winter. As trees and large bushes they need not be pruned much, simply thinned out occasionally. The Oriental Thorn becomes a pretty little tree about 15 ft high, and has very attractive fruits.

51   Crataegus oxyacantha punicea
Scarlet Hawthorn

Habitat: Europe and North Africa. This red variety of the common white thorn, together with the white thorn itself, are our most hardy and attractive thorn-bushes. The red flowers profusely in June, and the blossoms have a delightful scent.

Along with *Crataegus monogyna*, it is used in hedges. Indeed, thorn must be the most common hedge here, and it is the best, provided it is kept closely clipped and free from disease. It should preferably have a warm, chalky soil, rich in humus, and not permanently wet.

52   Crataegus oxyacantha
Paul's Scarlet

A fine, massively-flowering variety of No. 51, which does well either alone on a grass-plot or among low bushes. It reaches some 25 ft in height.

53   Crataegus crus-galli
Cockspur Thorn

Habitat: North America, The hard, sharp, slight-curved thorns, which are about 2 ins. long, have given this tree its name, It is to be recommended to anyone who wants an impassable hedge in the country. If it stands by itself, it becomes an attractive little tree with very vivid colouring in the autumn, and a mass of large, brilliant red haws. Grows about 12 ft high.

54   Cytisus praecox
Warminster Broom

Without a doubt the most prettily-growing of our brooms, and also extraordinarily profuse in its flowering, especially if in rather poor soil in the full sun. It is hardier than the common broom. It is often grown on large rock-gardens, among other low, flowering shrubs, and on the banks of terraces near the house. If it gets too large, it may be cut back severely after flowering, like common broom. It reaches some 5 ft in height and breadth.

55   Cytisus purpureus
Purple Broom

Habitat: North Italy. The variety *Cytisus purpureus incarnatus* is low-growing and creeping, and is seldom more than 18 ins. high. May be used as a ground cover between conifers, and has attractive purple pea-flowers about the beginning of June.

56   Cytisus kewensis
Kew Broom

Like the previous variety, this is of low, creeping habit with sulphur yellow flowers like No. 54. Useful for covering the ground on sunny banks.

57   Cytisus scoparius
Common Broom

Habitat: Europe. This familiar bush, whose yellow blooms appear on many railway embankments at the end of May, is especially suited for the driest and sunniest spots in a garden. It will flourish in rather difficult growing conditions, in a light sandy soil. A lovely, flower-covered bush.

Two points must be carefully watched,

however, if broom is to do well. It grows only when planted as a small seedling, or when sown direct; and it is necessary to cut the young plants right back after two or three years in succession, directly after they have flowered; otherwise instead of compact, delightful bushes, there will be those long, bare stems which are more often to be seen in gardens.

By means of crossing, many very beautiful varieties with large flowers and delightful colours have been produced. 'Andreanus' has flowers with yellow keels and brown standards. 'Firefly' has large vivid-yellow flowers with red streaks. 'Donard Seedling' has violet keels and orange standards, a remarkable colour-contrast of very great beauty.

Broom can grow to some 9 ft in height, but when pruned in the way just described remains at about half that heigth and are broad of growth.

58   Daphne mezereum
Mezereon

Habitat: Europe, Western Asia. If it is planted in a sheltered, sunny place, the *Daphne mezereum* will flower in February and March, making a cluster of small, sweet-scented mauve blooms. The leaves come later, and towards the end of the summer brilliant red berries develop. They are poisonous, and should be taken off at once, for fear of children eating them. It does well in ordinary, good garden-soil, in a place where there is some shade in the summer, and attains a height of 3 ft. Related to it is the lowgrowing, evergreen *Daphne cneorum*, which does best on a chalky, humus-rich soil, when it will flower prettily in June.

59   Davidia involucrata
Handkerchief Tree

Habitat: China. This tree grows in the most attractive manner, and has large vivid-green leaves, which resemble those of the lime. But its real glory is the bracts round the flowers, which have a remarkable beauty that is all their own. They are white and wing-shaped. The bracts and flowers are on long, slender stals, moving with the least breath of wind, so that the entire tree seems to be full of white doves, flapping their wings. Flowering seldom begins before the tree is ten years old.

It thrives in a light, porous soil, rich in humus, which should never become dry. It seems probable that the tree attains a height of nearly 50 ft, but as yet there is no certain knowledge of this since the tree is a newcomer. There are as yet very few specimens in Europe.

60   Deutzia rosea

Habitat: Japan. A low bush which becomes a mass of flowers. There are numerous lovely varieties. Extremely useful in the front of gardens, where a number of them should be planted together. Every three or four years all the oldest branches should be cut right down to the ground, so that the younger ones may flower freely. *Deutzia rosea campanulata* has pure white flowers. Both varieties attain no more than 5 ft in height. They flower in June of July.

61   Deutzia hybrida

A name that covers a number of attractive varieties, very free flowering and of a charming, compact, slightly pendant growth. 'Fleur de pommiers' is rose-coloured: 'Magicien' has large, frilled flowers of a pale violet shade: 'Mont Rose' has rose-coloured flowers and grow a little taller than the others.

62   Enkianthus campanulatus
Bell Bush

Habitat: Japan. A delightful bush with an unusual manner of growing, the branches forming horizontal tiers which give the effect of a pagoda. At the beginning of June the small, bell-shaped, creamy yellow, purple veined flowers appear. Together with the reddish new leaves, they give the whole bush a lovely glow of colour. It should stand unimpeded, among low-growing heathers for instance, in a porous loam, not exposed to wind. Grows about 6 ft high.

63 Elaeagnus commutata
Silver Berry

Habitat: North America. The silver-grey leaves can have a pretty appearance, but alongside lush, fresh-green bushes it can look very melancholy and dusty. It is best used with other easily-grown bushes in very windy and dry districts. *Elaeagnus multiflora* bears quite large, yellow fruits, which are edible. The bushes gow to about 14 ft.

64 Euonymus europaeus
Spindle Tree

Habitat: Europe. The great attraction of this plant, which is found wild in the British Isles, is its peculiar fruit, which lasts far into the winter. It tolerates a good deal of shade, and does well in almost any soil. Height, about 20 ft. *Euonymus alatus* is a variety with a remarkable, ribbed bark.

65 Erica vagans
Cornish Heath

Habitat: Europe. Not to be confused with Common Heather (*Calluna*), this is a very freely-flowering heather, which does well in any light soil, even if poor. The varieties, 'St. Keverne', which is rose-pink, and 'Mrs. D. F. Maxwell', which is deep cerise and dwarf, are more attractive than the species itself.

66 Erica carnea (herbacea)
Alpine Heath

Habitat: Southern Europe. A most beautiful and useful heather, which does well in light porous soil, rich in humus. In open positions, such as banks, it will blossom profusely.

67 Euonymus fortunei vegetus

Habitat: China. Attractive evergreen which is very suitable for planting between larger bushes and in poor light, for example in courtyards. It may be clipped. Height, some 3 ft.

68 Euonymus fortunei radicans

Habitat: China. Climbing, evergreen bush, which remains quite dwarf when it is left to grow along the ground; but it can climb admirably up walls and tree-trunks, just like ivy.
There is a pretty variety with mottled leaves, which maintain their handsome colour even in strong sunlight and dry conditions. The main variety will stand shade.

69 Fagus sylvatica
Common Beech

Habitat: Europe, including Britain. This lovely, woodland tree will do best in a chalky soil, containing much humus. The beech tolerates shade, but it attains its most characteristic colours and from when it is standing alone. For ordinary gardens it is far too greedy a tree. It makes a good hedge, however, and in both summer and winter is probably the most handsome of all living garden-walls. It should be planted in a chalky soil, and needs clipping twice a year, but it does not do well when subjected to severe cutting-back, or rejuvenation, as gardeners call it. It may also be planted in the middle of a group, since it can stand shade, or as a windbreak, when, it must be pruned every few years. The beech may grow to a height of nearly 80 ft, with almost as great a width at the crown.

70 Fagus sylvatica purpurea
Purple Beech (Copper Beech)

A tree which was planted in the middle of lawns by our grand-parents, but which is of doubtful value in the smaller gardens of the present time; both its size and its colour make it too dominating.

71 Fagus sylvatica laciniata
Cut-Leaved Beech

The leaves are very beautiful, but the tree should be used with caution, on account of its size, the amount of shade it gives, and its greedy nature.

72 Ficus carica
Common Fig Tree

Habitat: Mediterranean countries. Will thrive only in very sheltered, sunny localities, e.g. against a wall in a corner facing south-west, and will do best in the southern parts of the country.

The fig tree, however, has such beautiful and delicately drawn leaves that it is worth growing even when fruit cannot be obtained. Figs should not be pruned, but the top should be kept airy and open by moderate cutting back; they can be trained up a wall like other trellis trees, but will look more attractive if some of the branches are allowed to grow freely away from the wall.

73 Forsythia intermedia
Golden Bell

Habitat: China. Perhaps the favourite spring shrub of many gardens, where its abundant wealth of shining, yellow flowers glow among other pale green bushes in April-May. There are several varieties, making it possible to prolong the period of flowering. The earliest variety is *Forsythia ovata*, generally flo-

wering in the middle of April; it is no always as profusely flowering as th other varieties and is rather stiff in ha bit. Next come *Forsythia intermedia* an *Forsythia suspensa*. The former is th most richly blossoming and beautifull straight in habit. The latter has a stron tendency to droop, almost to trail, ma king it suitable for training up wall and arbours. A sub-variety named *For sythia suspensa fortunei* is stiffer and ha very large, pretty flowers.

Latest to bloom is *Forsythia viridissim* whose flowers, unlike those of the othe varieties, arrive simultaneously wit the leaves, which may dim the pu yellow glow of colour a little. Forsy thia should be pruned, i.e. older bran ches should be removed every fe years just after flowering.

74 Fraxinus excelsior
Common Ash

Habitat: Europe, Asia Minor. Ash doe best in calcareous, porous soil and i slow to start growing if planted in lawn. However, the tree will eventu ally grow very big, and is so greedy tha it is unsuitable for ordinary garden where the less vigorously growing *Fr xinus ornus* is preferable. This variet has very pretty, large, yellow-whit clusters of flowers around midsumme and attains a height of approximatel 26-32 ft. Common ash, on the othe hand, may reach a hight of 80-100 ft

75 Fuchsia riccartonii
Habitat: Chile. Most indoor fuchsia are not hardy enough for some garden and this variety may also be damage by frost. It is so pretty when in flowe however, and looks so light and grace ful that this risk should be taken. It ca be used in hedges, in groups in larg rock gardens, or along walls facin south. It flowers in late summer.

76 Genista tinctoria
Dyer's Greenweed

Habitat: Europe. Broom-like, small bush, flowering long and abundantly at the heigh of summer. It grows best on dry, soil in full sunlight and should be severly pruned every winter.

77 Ginkgo biloba
Maidenhair Tree

Habitat: China. The tree belongs to a family which was very rich in species in the Tertiary Age, but to-day the maidenhair tree is the only species left, and that only in cultivation. In many manor house gardens there is an attractive specimen, easily recognized by its straight and slender, pointed, conical top and the peculiar, bilobate leaves, reminiscent of the large, broad leaflets of the maidenhair fern.
Although the tree, in the course of 50-100 years, may attain up to 65 ft in height, it should nevertheless be possible to plant it in ordinary gardens by itself on a lawn, as it is so strangely beautiful; it may be possible to keep it a reasonable height by judicious cutting. It does not need special soil, but will not tolerate boggy or cold, wet soil.

78 Gleditsia triacanthos
Honey Locust

Habitat: North America. In many ways this resembles its relative, *Robinia*, False Acacia, or Locust Tree, but has very thin, serrulated, mimosa-like leaves appearing very late in the spring. Consequently, this tree is suitable among flowering, low shrubs and so-called woodland plants (primula, anemones, etc.). As it is unusually thorny, the thornless variety, *Gleditsia triacanthos inermis*, may be more suitable. It grows up to 40-50 ft high; it does best in warm, dry and light soil, and will not tolerate shade.

79 Halesia carolina
Snowdrop Tree

Habitat: North America. Handsome, flowering tree whose white, hanging flowers appear in May-June. Several trees may be planted together to form large groups and would look even more attractive with dwarfer, dense bushes around them. The Snowdrop Tree can reach 13-15 ft in height, and has no special demands as regards soil.

80 Hamamelis japonica
Japanese Witch Hazel

Habitat: Japan. The leaves resemble those of the hazel, but the flowers, appearing as early as January-February in mild winters, are quite unique and lovely, especially coming at an unusual time of year. The bush has a wide, crooked, picturesque habit, and must not be smothered by sturdier neighbouring shrubs. It can become 6-10 ft tall and 10-13 ft wide, and does best in deep soil, rich in humus, in a sheltered spot.

81 Helianthemum nummularium
Lawreson's Pink, Sun Rose

Habitat: Europe, Western Asia. Quite low, very richly flowering bushes which seldom attain more than 1-2 ft in height and so are most suitable for planting among rockery plants in sunny localities, on dry walls and on terraced slopes.
There are many pretty varieties and hybrids such as 'Ben Lui', with shining, red flowers and 'Ben Mare', with orange flowers.

82 Helianthemum nummularium
Golden Queen, Sun Rose

Cultivation and uses as for No. 81.

83 Hibiscus syriacus
Shrubby Mallow

Habitat: Central Asia. This has flowers

almost as beautiful as the well-known house plant of the same name. But it must be planted in a sheltered, sunny spot in a porous, sandy soil. Early in spring, any branches damaged by frost must be cut off, more or less as for an ordinary rose bush. In warm summers, flowering will begin in the middle of August, with a wealth of delightful flowers, right up to the arrival of frost in the autumn. There are several varieties, all with very pretty, vivid colours, e.g. '*Coelestis*', blue-violet; '*Comte de Flanders*', dark red; '*Jeanne d' Arc*', pure white; '*Ardens*', which is rose-coloured. Hibiscus will seldom grow taller than about 6 ft.

84 Hippophae rhamnoides
Sea Buckthorn

Habitat: Europe, Asia. Together with *Lycium barbarum* (No. 110) this bush is one of the toughest when it comes to resisting salt water spray and wind, and consequently is useful for planting in the dunes along our coasts. Under somewhat better conditions it will form delightful little trees, the female plants of which are covered with pretty, orange fruits in winter. Both male and female plants should always be planted. The staminate plants can be identified in winter by their thick buds. It can reach about 13-15 ft in height.

85 Holodiscus discolor

Habitat: North America. This bush, which may attain a height of 10-13 ft, is light and delicate in habit, and its clusters of flowers arrive in July. It is accommodating as far as soil is concerned, and will tolerate some shade.

86 Hydrangea arborescens
Tree Hydrangea

Habitat: North America. While many garden-owners are not particularly fond

of the somewhat pretentious and gaudy, large common garden hydrangea this variety will fit in more easily among other shrubs in the garden. The plant is more graceful and the yellow-white inflorescences not so large as those of the common garden variety. Old branches should be cut off every year or so and the tips of young ones should be slightly cut back. It reaches approximately 5 ft in height.

87 Hydrangea macrophylla
Hortensia Hydrangea

Habitat: Japan. It does best in rich non-calcareous humus, and will produce the greatest amount of flowers in a sunny locality. The variety '*Bouquet Rose*' flowers abundantly and is very hardy. The colour of the flowers may vary from pure rose to sky-blue, if the soil contains iron. It pays to cut off some of the oldest branches completely every few years and, in addition, to cut the young ones back a little at the tip.

88 Hydrangea paniculata
Plumed Hydrangea

Habitat: China, Japan. This ornamental shrub can reach up to 7 ft in height. It requires a very fertile soil, when it will flower quickly. As the clusters of flowers tend to become comparatively small after a few years, it is necessary to prune the previous year's growth right back every spring.

89 Hypericum calycinum
Rose of Sharon

Habitat: South Eastern Europe. One of the prettiest and most useful bushes for covering the ground among large shrubs. It spreads by suckers, and all that is necessary to obtain a compact green cover in quite a short time is to plant small rooted plants at intervals of about 8-13 ins.

t is partly evergreen and produces pretty, very large, yellow flowers in the late summer. If the leaves are damaged by frost, this will not kill the plant, but its top should be cut off right down near the ground.

90 Hypericum patulum henryi

Habitat: China. It will grow a little taller than the previous variety, and blossom profusely in late summer. It is not an evergreen, and will look best if pruned every spring.

91 Ilex pernyi
Perny's Holly

Habitat: China. A not very fast-growing holly with very prickly leaves. Its fruits are not so pretty as those of common holly (No. 93). This bush tolerates a certain amount of shade, and does well in city air, back gardens, etc., preferably in deep, non-calcareous soil, rich in humus.

92 Indigofera gerardiana
Shrubby Indigo

Habitat: Himalaya. This pretty little bush grows almost like a perennial and should be cut back severely every spring, whether it is frost-bitten or not.
In this manner, long, strong summer shoots are produced, which will terminate in many beautiful purple-violet pea flowers in the late summer. The locality should be dry and sunny, e.g. against a wall facing south. It will grow about 3 ft tall.

93 Ilex aquifolium
Common Holly

Habitat: Southern Europe. Holly may grow into a handsome, wide, conical tree about 19-25 ft. There are many attractive varieties, some with entire leaves and some with incised, very prickly leaves. There are very richly fruit-bearing female plants of the varieties, *Ilex aquifolium polycarpa*, and *Ilex a. pyramidailis*, and also varieties with yellow berries and mottled yellow leaves.

94 Juglans regia
Walnut

Habitat: South-eastern Europe and China. The common walnut is probably grown chiefly for its nice nuts, but where there is plenty of space, it will develop into a very handsome tree with curving branches in the winter and delightful, fragrant, beautifully carved leaves in the summer. Grafted, early-bearing varieties are preferable; they may bear fruit in 10-15 years. Walnut likes very porous, gravelly humus, fairly calcareous, and will do particularly well if the roots are watered frequently during the period of growth. It may grow 50-70 ft tall and equally wide. *Juglans ailantifolia* is a handsome walnut tree, less sturdy than *J. regia*, and with lovely, hanging clusters of nuts. Non-edible.

95 Kerria japonica pleniflora

Habitat: Japan. A small bush with delicate branches, blossoming prettily in May and then again late in summer. Its pale green branches look lovely in the garden in winter among other evergreen bushes.
Old branches should always be cut off after flowering. It will do best in a sunny spot in good compost. Height approximately 5 ft, or less if pruned.

96 Kalmia latifolia
Calico Bush

Habitat: North America. Typical acid-soil plant, i.e. does best in soil with very little lime, mixed with a fair amount of peat and leaf mould. In June pretty, delicate, pink flowers appear, growing in large umbels. It may form attractive, low evergreen bushes, suitable for planting in front of other acid-soil shrubs, such as rhododendron, etc. It will seldom grow more than 5 ft high.

97 Kolkwitzia amabilis
Beauty Bush

Habitat: China. Perhaps one of the best and most beautiful newly introduced flowering shrubs, light and graceful, and flowering profusely in June-July, particularly if cultivated in a sunny spot in fairly poor, light soil. It should not be hidden among other bushes, but planted by itself or in little groups on a lawn or among low bushes. Reaches 6-10 ft in height.

98 Laburnocytisus adamii

This peculiar tree is a so-called 'graft hybrid', i.e. it was produced accidentally by grafting purple broom on laburnum. Normally, no mixing occurs between two such grafted plants, but in this instance it did happen, and still happens whenever twigs from the original *Laburnocytisus adamii* are grafted onto the roots of ordinary laburnum.

The result is most interesting and not without a certain beauty when the tree or bush grows to maturity. As time goes by, the tree will produce branches bearing purple, upright clusters of 'broom', while the same branch may produce lovely, long, hanging, pure yellow clusters of laburnum. It should be planted by itself on a lawn in porous, calcareous soil and may attain up to 13-16 ft in height.

99 Lavandula spica
Lavender

Habitat: Southern Europe. Well-known, old-fashioned border plant with pretty, blue-violet, fragrant flowers in August. It can also be used as a small bush among rockery plants and dwarf bushes, and does best in warm,

light soil in a sunny locality. It should be clipped just after flowering.

100 Laburnum anagyroides
Golden Rain

Habitat: Southern Europe. With the lilac, probably the favourite flowering tree in many gardens. Correctly planted in order to allow it to develop freely in its singular, slightly overhanging way with a wealth of yellow, pendant clusters, it has a fairy-like beauty; often however, this tree is squeezed in among others, completely ruining its delicate shape. It does well in ordinary soil which may be a little poor and dry, but should not be soggy and wet. In the beginning of June the common laburnum starts to flower. *Laburnum alpinum* comes next, growing up to 25-30 ft tall with slightly longer clusters than the common laburnum; the longest clusters, of up to 1-2 ft are produced by the hybrid between these two varieties, i.e *Laburnum watereri vossii*. Laburnum does not need any pruning, only thinning and shaping. The seeds in the dry, brown pods are dangerous to children, who should be warned not to eat them. *Laburnum watereri vossii* will seldom produce seeds.

101 Ligustrum vulgare
Common Privet

Habitat: Europe, including Britain, and North Africa. Accommodating and useful shrub for hedges around the garden, as well as for planting among large shrubs and for sheltering zones, where conditions are too cold for the better *L. ovalifolium*. It does well in ordinary soil, in sun or shade, and produces dull white, heavily scented flowers followed by blue-black berries which remain on the bush all the winter, if not devoured by birds.

Where common privet is the only suitable plant, the variety *L. vulgare sem-*

pervirens is to be preferred. This is partly evergreen and makes a compact hedge up to 6 ft.

102 Ligustrum ovalifolium
Oval-leaved Privet

Habitat: Japan. Where a hedge is required, this is the species often used, but there are many better plants for the purpose.

Ligustrum obtusifolium regelianum (Habitat: Japan) is a low spreading variety, flowering abundantly in hot summers and with masses of lovely black berries in winter. It reaches about 3 ft in height. *L. sinense* of China is more satisfactory in Britain.

103 Ligustrum vulgare sempervirens

This is grown more often today than the common privet (No. 101) because its foliage is prettier and it stays green in mild winters.

104 Liriodendron tulipifera
Tulip Tree

Habitat: North America. A striking tree with strangely shaped leaves and beautiful tulip-like flowers, appearing in July. It does best in porous, warm, calcareous soil as a specimen in a sheltered garden.

Although in time the tree may grow very tall (up to 100 ft), it is nevertheless worth planting, as it can be kept to a reasonable size by judicious shaping. It takes on a particularly strong, yellow autumn hue.

105 Lonicera maackii podocarpa
Shrubby Honeysuckle

Habitat: Korea. A pretty bush which may reach some 6 ft in height and should be planted especially for its very lovely, bright red fruits. It will thrive in ordinary soil.

106 Lonicera pileata
Box Honeysuckle

Habitat: Western China. This and the following *Lonicera* are semi-evergreen, with delicate branches and a low, wide habit, rendering them most suitable for planting in front of shrubberies and among evergreen bushes. It reaches 1-2 ft in height and will tolerate some cutting-back if damaged by frost.

The variety *Lonicera pileata yunnanensis* (*L. nitida fertilis*) has a pretty, slightly pendant habit, and in sunny localities will produce many lovely, violet-blue berries.

107 Lonicera nitida
Chinese Honeysuckle

Habitat: Western China. This is slightly taller than the previous variety.

108 Lonicera syringantha
Shrubby Honeysuckle

Habitat: North-western China. A very richly flowering bush which, in full sunlight and good soil, will reach up to 8 ft in height and in June produce a wealth of small, violet, fragrant flowers.

109 Lonicera tatarica
Tartarian Honeysuckle

Habitat: Southern Russia. Sturdy, robust and unexciting bush, perhaps not particularly pretty, but useful for giving shelter and filling up in large shrubberies. *Lonicera tatarica rosea* or *rubra* is better and will produce many attractive, rose-coloured flowers in May-June and red, currant-like berries in winter.

110 Lycium barbarum
Box Thorn

Habitat: Southern Europe. This is the bush which will tolerate best the severe conditions along the coasts as it is not damaged by salt sea water. It is suitable for dry slopes, where it spreads by runners, and should only be in the conditions described. It may grow up to 6-10 ft tall.

111 Magnolia obovata

Habitat: China and Japan. This is grown mainly for its white, fragrant flowers and its large, beautiful leaves, which may reach up to $\frac{1}{2}$-1 ft in length. *Magnolia tripetala* (known in England as the 'Umbrella Tree'), has still larger leaves, up to about 2 ft long. Height 25-30 ft.

112 Magnolia sieboldii

Habitat: Japan. This does not have as many flowers as the following two varieties, but is the most attractive. The simple, water-lily-like, snowy white flowers are of an indescribably noble shape and of almost spiritual beauty. Does best by itself in non calcareous, porous soil, rich in humus, in a warm and sheltered spot among large, evergreen trees. It may reach 6-10 ft in height.

113 Magnolia soulangiana

To many garden owners, this flowering spring tree seems the most beautiful thing one can possess, and not without reason. But the delightful, large, tulip-like flowers should be seen against a dark, quiet background of evergreen bushes and not, as is often the case, against a red brick wall, ruining the effect of the delicate pink of its charming flowers. It should be planted in good, ordinary, porous garden soil; and should not be pruned. It may reach a height of 13-16 ft.

There are varieties with pure white and rose-violet flowers.

114 Magnolia stellata
Star Flowered Magnolia

Habitat: Japan. Flowers very profuse-ly and is the earliest variety to blossom in mild winters it may be in full flowe as early as March, with an abundance of small, snowy-white, star-shaped flowers. It may attain a height of up to 6 ft but grows slowly. A somewha taller variety, growing into a small tree is *Magnolia kobus*, but it must reach 8-10 years of age before it will begin to flower.

115 Mahonia aquifolium
Oregon Grape

Habitat: North America. Evergreen low bush, spreading by underground shoots, and consequently well suited for planting among other, taller evergreen bushes, or in front of large groups .The yellow clusters of flowers arrive early in May, and in the autumn this bush has large, pretty, grape-like bunches of berries which look charming among the prickly, glossy leaves The bush may be cut back severely, and this will produce many young, red shoots of a very pleasing hue. Height approximately 3-5 ft, unless cut back every year.

116 Malus floribunda
Flowering Crab

Habitat: Japan. All crab trees are very pretty and useful for small gardens, for which it is hard to find trees which will not grow too large. They would look nice as specimens on the lawn or with other bushes in the front garden, where they give the entire road a festive look in the spring. The trees can be bought in the shape of ordinary bushes or standards. The height varies up to over 6 ft. In many instances a young bush specimen will grow into a handsome tree with many slightly crooked trunks of much better effect than one long, straight trunk. The soil should be as for ordinary apple trees, i.e. good deep soil, rich in humus, without stag nant water in winter. Pruning should consist of a suitable thinning-out of the branches at an interval of a few years, always done in such a manner as to maintain the natural shape of the top. The tree will flower in the middle of May and may reach up to 20-24 ft in height.

117 Malus 'John Downie'
Crab Apple

'John Downie' was raised near Lichfield, England, and is perhaps the best crab apple for making preserves, but the fruit is too sour for people to eat raw. Height 20-24 ft.

118 Malus halliana
Flowering Crab

Cultivated in Japan and China. This has fairly large, delicately shaped flowers with lovely buds. Light and airy of habit, and grows some 13-16 feet in height.

119 Malus eleyi
Flowering Crab

A hybrid raised by Mr. Charles Eley of Suffolk, England. Charming, light tree with great clusters of violet-red flowers and purplish red fruits. The young leaves are purple. Height 13-16 ft.

120 Malus scheideckeri
Flowering Crab

A hybrid. One of the most abundantly flowering and finest crab-trees, with rose-coloured, double flowers and small, exquisite, yellow fruits, remaining on the tree far into the winter to the delight of birds. Height 10-13 ft.

Among other nice-looking crab-trees may be mentioned *Malus arnoldiana* which is particularly low, wide and almost creeping in habit, and has a wealth of light rose-coloured flowers and yellow fruits. *Malus sargentii*, of Japan is also a large, wide tree of some

6 ft in height, but has white flowers. *Malus spectabilis* from China grows into a comparatively tall tree of some 13-16 ft, and has pretty, pink, full flowers and yellow fruits.

121 Mespilus germanica
Medlar

Habitat: Europe and Turkey. Quite a strange little tree with large, brown, decorative fruits in winter; the leaves take on a very pretty, red autumn hue. The fruits can be eaten fresh after they have become soft. It may grow up to 13-16 ft. high.

122 Morus nigra
Black Mulberry

Habitat: Probably Western Asia. It should always be planted in a warm corner facing south-west or against a wall in very porous soil, rich in humus. Large branches should be trained against the wall, but pruning must be done very carefully and only when strictly necessary. This tree heals badly, and the branches are very brittle and easily broken at the forks; consequently isolated trees must be carefully supported by forked, vertical stakes when full of fruit. The fruits must be completely reddish-black before they are ready to eat.

123 Pernettya mucronata

Habitat: Chile. Low, up to about 1½ ft tall, small, evergreen bushes, producing very pretty, white, pink or violet-coloured berries. They should be used among ericaceous plants which will thrive only in non-calcareous soil. (Rhododendron, Calluna, etc)

124 Paeonica suffruticosa
Tree Peony

Habitat: North-western China. It may grow into a bush about 6 ft in height with a wealth of magnificent, large paeony flowers, more beautiful in colour and shape than ordinary perennial paeonies, but easily damaged by late frost. It should be planted in a sunny spot in a good, well-drained soil, mixed with lime. There are many wonderful varieties.

125 Pieris japonica

Habitat: Japan, Charming, evergreen shrub with shiny, dark green leaves and, in the spring, very pretty, mahogany-red young leaves at the lips of the shoots, together with white, light tassels of flowers. It likes light shade in non-calcareous soil. Grows up to 10 ft high.

126 Philadelphus coronarius
Mock Orange

Habitat: Southern Europe. This species has a very strong fragrance, but is otherwise not particularly pretty and should be grown only for filling out in large shrubberies, where it will tolerate some shade and poor soil. It may grow up to 10 ft in height.

127 Philadelphus *hybrid*
Mock Orange

This name applies to some very pretty varieties with large flowers, some of them scented, some non-scented, which are well worth growing. They do best and flower most abundantly in the sun in fairly poor soil, but may also become pretty in half-shade. One of the best, tall varieties is '*Virginal*', with large, pure white, sweet-scented flowers. Height up to 10ft.
Among the medium-tall varieties may be mentioned '*Voie Lactee*' with particularly large flowers of a pure white colour and pretty, yellow-orange stamens. '*Bouquet Blanc*' has double, delightful, white flowers and a slightly pendant, graceful habit. Among the dwarf varieties, reaching only 3-5 ft in

height, may be pointed out '*Mont Blanc*' wide and sturdy and with a wealth of very strongly scented flowers; '*Girandole*', of approximately the same shape and height, and with large, double, milk-white flowers. All *Philadelphus* varieties flower during the month of June.

128 Platanus hispanica
London Plane

A hybrid of Asian and N. American species. Very handsome, large tree with peculiar bark peeling off in sections on trunk and branches when old. It can be grown only where there is plenty of space, as the tree will reach up to 65-80 ft in height.

129 Populus alba
White Poplar

Habitat: Southern Europe and Asia. Most poplars are strong growing, unexacting, but greedy trees, draining the garden soil of nourishment and water. They should therefore be grown with care and only in conditions where it is essential to create shelter in a short time, or in gardens where other, more handsome and fine trees cannot thrive owing to strong winds. The white poplar may reach up to 100 ft in height.

130 Populus canescens *Grey Poplar*

Habitat: Europe and Western Asia. Its large, strong top shows up to magnificent effect in the landscape, but the tree is greedy and has the bad habit of sending up suckers at a great distance from the trunk. It attains 65-80 ft.

131 Populus berolinensis
Berlin Poplar

This hybrid variety of poplar is enormously fast-growing and can put out shoots of more than a yard in one summer. It is excellently suited for fast-growing, sheltering hedges and will tolerate severe cutting-back every winter It will produce many suckers at a great distance from the plant.

132 Populus lasiocarpa
Red-veined Poplar

Habitat: Western China. One of the slowest-growing varieties of poplar. This makes it suitable for ordinary gardens, if one likes a tree with the characteristic large leaves responsible for its Danish name, Rhubarb Poplar.

133 Populus nigra italica
Lombardy Poplar.

Habitat: Europe and Western Asia. These picturesque and romantic-looking trees, which often used to be found in old parks, should be planted only where there is plenty of space, as they are greedy and will send out a lot of suckers in all directions. They will grow 50-65 ft tall.

134 Populus tremula
Aspen

Habitat: Europe, North Africa and Turkey. As a sheltering tree and in difficult, exposed conditions, quite an excellent, hardly and unexacting type. The perpetual quivering and movement of the leaves at the least breath of wind has given the tree its name. It can reach up to 80 ft in height.

135 Potentilla fruticosa
Shrubby Cinquefoil

Habitat: Northern Europe, Asia and America. All the varieties and hybrids of this species are about 3 ft tall, charming, richly flowering, small bushes, in flower all through the summer. They thrive in ordinary, good garden soil in a sunny locality, and are well suited for growing in front of groups or among other small flowering shrubs, or perhaps as small hedges not requiring trimming. At annual intervals, a considerable cutting-back will result in fresh new growth and improved flowering.

136 Potentilla fruticosa farreri
Shrubby Cinquefoil

Pretty, pure yellow-flowering species, together with the variety, *Potentilla fruticosa farreri prostrata*, which is low and almost creeping.

137 Potentilla fruticosa veitchii
Shrubby Cinquefoil

One of the most rapidly growing varieties with pretty, grey-green leaves which look charming against the pale yellow flowers.

138 Prunus dulcis *Almond*

In a warm, sunny locality in warm, porous and calcareous soil an almond tree will look perfectly delightful when it comes into flower in March. In good summers, the thick-skinned almond fruits will ripen. It should be pruned with great care and only moderately thinned out in late summer. May grow 13-16 ft high.

139 Prunus avium plena
Double Gean

Habitat: Europe, Western Asia. A very fast-growing, ornamental tree which will not produce berries owing to its double flowers.

140 Prunus cerasifera pissardii
Purple-leaved Plum

Habitat: Western Asia, Caucasus. Dark red leaves and pink flowers make this small tree or large bush charming, although it should not be planted against a red house, etc., where the dominant red colour of the leaves will easily clash. It will grow some 13-16 ft.

141 Prunus laurocerasus
Cherry Laurel

Habitat: Southern Europe and Asia Minor. Evergreen bushes doing well in the shade, though not under large trees and bushes. It will tolerate cutting-back after frost-bite in hard winters, and can attain 10-13 ft in height. The narrow-leaf varieties, *Prunus Laurocerasus shipkaensis* and *zabeliana*, are Broader of habit and hardier than the species itself.

142 Prunus padus *Bird Cherry*

Habitat: Europe, Western Asia, and Japan. This pretty little tree with its delicate, pale-green foliage and wealth of white, fragrant clusters of flowers in May, is one of the most delightful wild trees. It will also do well in half-shade, and may become 20-25 ft tall. In the garden the form '*watereri*' and the double *plena* are to be preferred.

143 Prunus spinosa
Sloe

Habitat: Europe and Western Asia. The reason why the common wild sloe is included is its accommodating nature and great hardiness in strong winds. As a sheltering hedge around a garden in the country, exposed to strong winds, it will do particularly well, and at the same time its thorny, tangled habit will form an impenetrable hedge. It is best planted as a small plant in a dry, sunny locality.

144 Prunus tenella
Dwarf Russian Almond

Habitat: South-Eastern Europe and Western Asia. It will spread vigorously by suckers and should be planted among large, light trees or evergreen bushes, where it can spread in peace. Flowers abundantly in May and reaches about 3 ft in height.

145 Prunus 'Amanogawa'
Japanese Cherry

Habitat: China and Japan. A tall ornamental tree of fastigiate habit which should preferably be planted by itself on a lawn or among low bushes. It will look effective also against a background of dark, evergreen bushes. It flowers in May and may reach a height of 13-20 ft.

146 Prunus 'Hisakura'
Japanese Cherry

Habitat: China, Japan. Whereas there are several handsome trees which are planted in our gardens far too seldom, this tree is planted almost too often. The Japanese cherry trees can have an overpowering effect when there are great masses of coloured bloom along some suburban roads in May time. The pure pink flowers of the varieties which follow are not so strong in effect but the '*Hisakura*' variety has a strange, bluish-pink colour which clashes, with the reddish-brown young leaves. The tree has a stiff habit, not at all graceful. If these trees are planted as avenue-trees leading up to a charming old farmhouse, they will make a very strange impression in the countryside. It may reach 16-20 ft in height and may be grown both as a tree with a tall trunk and as a bush.

147 Prunus 'Shirotae' (*Mount Fuji*)
Japanese Cherry

Habitat: China and Japan. Among the many varieties of Japanese cherry trees this is one of the prettiest, bearing delightful, large, pendant, white flowers on almost horizontal boughs.
Another variety with a vigorous habit is '*Shidare Sakura*', with large, pure pink, double flowers. It should always be planted as a standard.

148 Prunus subhirtella
Spring Cherry

Habitat: Japan. Towards the end of April, this big Japanese bush is completely covered with a wealth of small pink flowers, and looks lovely among other early Spring bushes. Height, approx. 9 to 12 ft. Another variety *Prunus subhirtella autumnalis* bears beautiful flowers in December if the weather is mild. There is also a pendant type, which looks lovely when grown as a standard; it is called *Prunus subhirtella pendula*

149   Prunus triloba
Flowering Almond

Habitat: China. This flowering bush is much favoured by garden owners, and with good reason, as it is pretty when full of rose-pink buds ready to burst in March-April. Unfortunately, this lovely state lasts for a very short time and, moreover, the bush is often attacked by a fungus disease, which may kill large sections of the branches. Severe pruning immediately after the end of flowering is the best means of defeating the attacks. It grows approximately 4-6 ft tall.

150   Pterocarya fraxinifolia
Wing Nut

Habitat: Caucasus. A very handsome tree, unfortunately too large for planting in ordinary gardens. It can be grown in a large front garden if pruned with care, without destroying its characteristic shape. The attractive, pinnate leaves and the strange, hanging flowers and fruits give the tree an exotic look. It may reach a height of 50-65 ft.

151   Ptelea trifoliata
Hop Tree

Habitat: North America. It grows as a high, sturdy bush or small tree of about 10 ft, with pretty, leathery, green leaves and peculiar-looking seed vessels in autumn.

152   Pyracantha coccinea
Firethorn

Habitat: South Europe, Turkey. Few

bushes have become as widespread as this in gardens during the last generation. The main reason why it has become so popular is its rowan-berry-like, shining, orange berries, growing in thick clusters along all the old branches of the bush. Particularly if grown against the south wall of the house, or on terraced slopes facing south, it will produce a wealth of great clusters of berries, which may remain far into the autumn, provided the birds will leave them alone. It may grow level with the first floor, but does not need pruning, only tying back and cutting off superfluous branches. The variety *Pyracantha coccinea lalandii* has larger fruits than the species.

153   Quercus rubra
Red Oak

Habitat: North America. Oaks are too tall and vigorous to be suitable for ordinary gardens, but *Quercus rubra* is one of the most useful kinds, as it will not grow very tall and will also tolerate pruning. It looks magnificent in autumn, when its large, leathery leaves will turn dark-red and bronze. Its height averages some 60-80 ft.

154   Quercus robur
English Oak

Habitat: Europe, Turkey. This common oak, growing in the forests, can hardly develop fully and handsomely in an ordinary garden, but in large country gardens the oak might still be planted. The soil should be deep with humus and the locality open and not exposed to strong winds.

155   Rhamnus frangula
Alder Buckthorn

Habitat: Europe, North Africa and Western Asia. Small, shade-tolerating tree with shiny, green leaves and nice, red fruits, which will do best in slightly damp soil, rich in humus, and will reach a height of 13-16 ft.

156 Rhododendron catawbiense

Habitat: Eastern North America. Seldom grown in British gardens, but is the parent of some of the best very hardy hybrids. All rhododendrons require a lime free soil, which should not be dry or heavy. A peaty, leafy soil is the best, but a moist sandy loam is almost as good. After planting, the roots should be watered often, particularly during the period of flowering, and after flowering all withered clusters of flowers should be picked off without breaking the new shoots. The plants must never be allowed to dry around the roots, and frost must not be permitted to penetrate too deeply into the soil; this is prevented by covering the surface between the plants with compost and mown grass from the lawns and old manure. The earth between rhododendrons must never be dug with a spade.

Rhododendrons will look prettiest when many of them are placed together in groups on a lawn, or on the fringe of an evergreen shrubbery; they will prefer some shade, but not overhanging branches. When old, they may reach a height of up to 10 ft.

157 Rhododendron 'Parsons Gloriosum'

Flowers early in June, is hardy and of vigorous habit.

158 Rhododendron 'Caractacus'

Comparatively late-flowering, vigorously growing variety with shining, red flowers. 'Dr. V. H. Rutgers' is also a pretty red, but of dwarf habit.

159 Rhododendron 'Pink Pearl'

Vigorously-growing variety with very large flowers.

160 Rhododendron 'Rosamundii'

Flowers very early (by the end of March), and is low and dense in habit. The variety *Roseum elegans* is rather like it and also very early.

161 Rhododendron ferrugineum
Alpen Rose

Habitat: The Central European Alps. Low, evergreen shrub with charming, small, red flowers. It is not always very easy to make this real 'rose of the alps' blossom in cultivation. On the other hand, there is a cross between this and another wild variety *R. hirsutum*, called *Rhododendron halense*, which will flower more abundantly and is easier to cultivate.

162 Rhododendron 'Princess Marika'

Cultivation as above.

163 Rhododendron
Mollis Azalea type

There are many wonderful species and varieties in beautiful colours of this azalea: shining yellow, fiery red, and salmon orange. Many have pretty names, with the common name, *Rhododendron molle hybrida*. They grow like ordinary rhododendrons but will not become so tall, and lose their leaves in the autumn, after turning a beautiful red or yellow. Along the edge of a lake or a pond, these richly flowering bushes will look wonderful in May, when their flowers are reflected in the water. Soil, etc, as for rhododendron (No. 156).

164 Rhododendron
Ghent Azalea type

Like the previous shrub, a richly flowering and colourful bush with many varieties in delightful colours; orange yellow, pale pink, pale yellow, and glowing orange red. The earliest will flower in May.

165 Rhododendron praecox

A hybrid between *R. ciliatum* and *R. dauricum*. As early as the end of February and the beginning of March this small, semi-evergreen variety of rhododendron may flower and light up the garden with its shining, purple flowers. It should be planted in a sheltered locality, and will grow about 3 ft tall.

166 Rhododendron schlippenbachii

Habitat: Korea and Japan. The large, delicately pink, faintly scented flowers arrive in April-May. It reaches a height of about 5 ft.

167 Rhus typhina laciniata
Cut-leaved Stag's Horn Sumach

Habitat-North America. In many ways a strange and beautiful small tree or large bush, which will look most decorative if planted by itself or in groups against a modern house. In winter especially the peculiar fruits of the female and the delicate tracery of the branches will look lovely against a light wall. It can be grown by itself on a lawn, but should not be mixed with other, larger bushes. It will reach 13-16 ft in height and in autumn will produce pretty, scarlet leaves in a sunny, dry locality.

168 Rhus typhina
Stag's Horn Sumach

Uses and growing instructions as above. Both may sucker in suitable soil.

169 Ribes sanguineum
Flowering Currant

Habitat: North America. One of the popular spring shrubs which, when used with moderation, looks nice together with Forsythia and Prunus. *Ribes sanguineum splendens* is a variety with particularly large, deep red clusters of flowers. It may grow 6-10 ft tall,

is unexacting and will tolerate light shade.

170 Ribes alpinum
Alpine Currant

Habitat: Europe. Unexacting and unobtrusive bush which, because of its very early leafing and its pretty, compact, delicate branches and great ability to tolerate shade and bad growing conditions among old trees and high bushes, deserves attention and should be preferred where other, perhaps prettier, shrubs will not thrive. The flowers are insignificant, small and greenish, but the pale green leaves are so attractive and charming that they alone render the bush lovely enough. It reaches a height of 5-7 ft at most, and an equal width. It should not be pruned, but could be shaped now and then.

171 Ribes odoratum
Buffalo Currant

Habitat: North America. An easily grown shrub for large groups which has yellow, sweet-scented flowers in May. Grows to about 7 ft high.

172 Robinia pseudoacacia decaisneana
False Acacia

Habitat: North America. Very handsome, light and delicately leafy tree which will not give much shade for bushes and other plants growing at its base. If planted near the terrace of the house, or in the front garden, it will look very pretty against the building, owing to its picturesque, gnarled branches. At the end of June the flowers appear, and the tree looks most attractive when the clusters of delicate pink are suspended from nearly every branch and twig. A warm locality with much sun, and porous, calcareous soil are the conditions for good growth. The tree must be supported right up to its top for the first few years, and should be cut back now and then in order to create a stiff crown, as the branches are liable to break. It may reach a height of 65-80 ft.

173 Rosa canina *Dog Rose*

Habitat: Europe. As the first of a number of delightful, wild species of roses, or 'shrub roses' as they are often called, there is the local wild dog-rose, and what is said about this rose concerning soil, pruning and uses, also applies to the other wild roses mentioned, up to No. 186. All these roses are quite unexacting as regards soil and nourishment. They will flower and do best in porous loam, and do not like boggy, damp or low positions or cold soil. If placed by themselves in the sun they will become much prettier both in shape and blossom than if squeezed between other bushes in a thicket. In the country, they look lovely in a hedge by themselves, planted perhaps at the top of a low stone wall.

In small gardens, it should be remembered that most varieties of wild roses need a lot of space, as they will often reach some 7 ft or more in top diameter. On or two groups of 3-6 bushes planted by themselves on the law would be enough in many cases, and in any event, this will give these pretty bushes the best opportuinity for development and shape.

Pruning is generally unadvisable, in fact, the shortening of the long, young, summer shoots especially, would be vandalism, as these gracefully overhanging, curving branches are the very ones where flowers will appear the year after; a suitable thinning-out of old, worn-out branches, i.e. cutting them off right down near the ground, might be useful, but the wide, slightly pendent habit of these bushes must always be kept in mind. If they grow too wide for their position, this is simply because the wrong kind of bush has been chosen, and cutting back will not help matters. They grow up to 10 ft high.

174 Rosa carolina
Carolina

Habitat: North America. Low-growing, only about 3 ft in height, spreading by suckers. Charming, pink flowers in great clusters and a great amount of hips in winter. Excellent for slopes and for planting among taller species.

175 Rosa heleneae
Helen Wilson's Rose

Habitat: Central China. Quite a charming bush rose with long, curved branches, bearing many flowered panicles of white fragrant flowers in June. It has small red hips and grows to about 3 ft high.
(For growing instructions, see No. 173).

176 Rosa foetida
Austrian Briar

Habitat: Western Asia. Old-fashioned, well-known garden rose, whose subspecies and varieties especially should be grown to-day.
Some of the most delightful are: '*Jaune bicolor*'; single yellow with a coppery outside: '*Persian Yellow*', with double, glowing, yellow flowers. '*Harrison's Yellow*' is double, too, and of a warm ochre yellow. These roses blossom only once, in June; the plants reach a height of 3-5 ft, and need a warm, sheltered position.

177 Rosa moyesii
Shrub Rose

Habitat: N.W. China. Tall and erect of habit, with long, sturdy branches which may reach up to 10 ft in length.

The lovely flowers with their characteristic, deep-red colour and the long, bottle-shaped hips make this bush rose one of the most beautiful.

178 Rosa hugonis
Shrub Rose

Habitat: Central China. Very pretty in shape and covered in June with a wealth of pale yellow flowers. Black or dark-born hips come later. Height approximately 7 ft.

179 Rosa omeiensis pteracantha
Red Thorn Mt Omei Rose

Habitat: Western China. Unusually large, red thorns on the young boughs make this wild rose particularly pretty, all the more so as it has very delicate leaves and lovely, white flowers. It is especially suited as a hedge round a country garden.

180 Rosa omeiensis
Mt Omei Rose

Habitat: China. It does not have quite as large thorns as the foregoing variety. It flowers in May and may reach a height of 4-7 ft.

181 Rosa rugosa
Ramanas Rose

Habitat: Japan and Northern China. The hardiest and most easily-grown wild rose imaginable. It will even grow in very severe conditions in gardens along the coasts, where it will spread luxuriantly even in poorest and sandy soil.

Its large, pretty hips are very good to eat, and due to their large content of vitamins, they are called the 'oranges of the north' in Scandinavian countries. Through crossings with other roses, varieties have been created with larger flowers in several delightful colours. One of the prettiest is that illustrated, *'Dagmar Hastrup'*, and the white *'Stella Polaris'*, both with quantities of large hips. Among double varieties with comparatively small flowers may be mentioned, *'Signe Relander'* which is dark red, *'Grootendorst'*, crimson, and *'Grootendorst Pink'*, pink. All three have flowers in large umbels and may reach 3-7 ft in height.

182 Rosa rubiginosa
'Lady Penzance', *Sweet Briar*

Habitat: Europe. This hybrid of the wild sweet briar has retained the fine, sharp apple scent of the species and, in addition, has inherited its delightful, copper flowers from *Rosa foetida*, with which it was crossed. The variety *'Lucy Bertram'* is also a hybrid, whose characteristics are attractive, glowing red flowers and a scent of apples.

183 Rosa spinosissima *variety*
Scotch or Burnet Rose

Habitat: Europe and N. Asia. Comparatively low, delicately branched bush, growing in the wild state on sand dunes very hardy and charming. The varieties *Rosa spinosissima altaia* and *Rosa spinosissima hispida* have large, whitish-yellow and lemon-yellow flowers, respectively, and are better suited for planting in ordinary gardens. It will flower in May-June and reach 3½ ft in height.

184 Rosa blanda
Smooth or Meadow Rose

Habitat: North America. Light and delicate habit with large, rose-coloured flowers in May-June. It may reach up to 7 ft in height.

185 Rosa centifolia muscosa
Moss Rose

A sport of the Cabbage Rose, which may be a hybrid. These graceful, old-fashioned, poetic roses are still worth growing, although they will only flower abundantly once at the height of summer.

Both on stems and sepals there is a peculiar, moss-like, hairy coating which has given these roses their name. In England, in the nineteenth century, a great number of delightful varieties were grown with abundantly full flowers and a charming, delicate fragrance. Among suitable varieties used now might be mentioned 'Common Red Moss Rose' and 'Cristata', both of a pure pink colour; 'Reine Blanche', which is white and, in addition, 'Eugenie Guinoisseau', purplish-violet, and 'Salet', which is rose-coloured. The latter two will flower once or twice again in the late summer.

186 Rosa borboniana
Bourbon Rose

Probably the most beautiful of all old-fasioned roses, and a delightful, luxuriant and richly flowering bush which grows up to 6 ft.

187 Hybrid Perpetual Rose 'General Jacqueminot'

Following the above-mentioned wild roses, we now come to a number of so-called 'improved' roses, i.e. roses which, for various reasons which cannot be explained here, have been created by hybridising.

The pruning cannot be described here in detail, but in short consists of cutting off all withered and dead twigs to fresh buds in the spring, and of cutting back all fresh, year-old branches a little (about one-third of branch) in the group of roses flowering several times during the season, while roses of the Hybrid Tea and Pernetiana groups (see No. 191 and following), are pruned more severely every year, up to about a half of the year-old branches. Finally, the Hybrid Polyantha roses, or Floribundas (see No. 210 and onwards), can be very

severely cut back; in many cases two thirds of the year-old branches can be removed.

All improved roses with large flower should preferably be planted in fresh porous loam which has been previously dug particularly deep down, up to nearly two spits, and perhaps given some peat mould and old cow dung down to about one spit. The rose should be planted fairly deep down with the budded point slightly *below* the surface; then the subsoil should be watered and the rose pruned fairly severely the first time. In summer, the soil should be kept permanently loose with a cultivator, and a little ammonium sulphate should be given once or twice during the early summer. Dead flowers should be removed at once with a small piece of stem for perpetual roses and a long piece of stem in the case of polyantha roses. Disease control should be done as a prevention and not as a cure, as the latter will often be too late. Consequently, the roses should be dusted or sprayed *before* the onset of mildew or leaf spot, etc. *'General Jacqueminot'* is a sturdy plant and may reach 3 ft and more in height, so that it and other varieties of the same group should not be planted in small or long, narrow borders, but in a large, circular bed or in front of a shrubbery. These roses have fairly short stems, but a lovely fragrance, and will often go on flowering far into the late summer.

188 Hybrid Perpetual Rose 'Mrs. John Laing'

Very vigorously growing and sound, as well as being one of the most handsome and richly blossoming of these old-fashioned roses.

189 Hybrid Perpetual Rose 'Frau Karl Druschki'

Delightful, white variety, flowering

unusually long in the autumn, but without much scent.

190 Hybrid Perpetual Rose 'Charles Bonnet'

Luxuriant and richly flowering variety with lovely fragrance.

191 Hybrid Tea Rose 'Geheimrat Duisberg'

This group of roses had been named after a well-known French rose grower, who has produced a number of delightful roses with large flowers in yellow and orange colours. They all have glossy, sound leaves. The above-mentioned variety will flower abundantly and is fragrant. For cultivation, see No. 187.

192 Hybrid Tea Rose 'New Yorker'

One of the loveliest of red roses. Keeps its red colour well and is fragrant.

193 Hybrid Tea Rose 'Betty Uprichard'

Sound, richly blossoming variety, flowering far into the late summer. Lovely scent.

194 Hybrid Tea Rose 'Dainty Bess'

Unusual, light and lovely, but with little fragrance.

195 Hybrid Tea Rose 'Dame Edith Helen'

Probably one of the best, strongly scented, rose-coloured varieties for large flowers borders.

196 Hybrid Tea Rose 'Edina'

Extremely elegant shape, dazzlingly white in colour and lovely fragrance.

197 Hybrid Tea Rose 'Eclipse'

Vigorous and richly blossoming with very long, elegantly shaped, strongly scented flowers.

198 Hybrid Tea Rose 'Peace'

Seldom in the recent past has there appeared such an inimitably delightful rose as this. Sound, luxuriant, with attractive, shiny, dark-green leaves, lovely fragrance and very large, very full, beautifully shaped flowers, changing in colour from pure yellow with a little red in the bud stage to the most delicate pink with a golden hue in the flower in full bloom. It does not wither in a depressing manner with brown, curled-up petals, but when at its most beautiful, all the petals will suddenly fall.

The plant is fairly tall and sturdy, and this kind should not be planted together with other, more delicate varieties.

199 Hybrid Tea Rose 'Picture'

Along with 'Dame Edith Helen' one of the prettiest and best pale pink varieties and, moreover, sound and fragrant.

200 Hybrid Tea Rose 'Spek's Yellow'

Brightly glowing. Pure yellow and fragrant, of delicate, but luxuriant habit.

201 Hybrid Tea Rose 'Talisman'

Of very special beauty, when in bud as the flower is very long and elegant, with yellow and copper red hues and tracery. On the other hand, it is so vigorous in habit and so full of flower that many flowers in full bloom may give the flower border an untruly look.

202 Hybrid Tea Rose 'Ena Harkness'

Along with the 'New Yorker' variety, this fairly new rose, of a clear, dark red, is one of the best in the dark-coloured group.

The plant is vigorous and sound in habit and the flowers very pretty in bud. They will retain their red colour right up to the point of falling. Enchanting fragrance.

203 Hybrid Tea Rose 'Etoile de Hollande'

Pretty, dark red and very sweet-scented variety which, unfortunately, has the slight draw-back that its flowers will grow purple when old. It has a lovely scent, however, and is otherwise an excellent hardy rose.

204 Hybrid Tea Rose 'Edith Nelly Perkins'

Delicately and elegantly shaped, pointed flower of luxuriant habit.

205 Hybrid Tea Rose 'Elite'

A rose of vigorous habit, blossoming abundantly, but with only a faint fragrance.

206 Hybrid Tea Rose 'Flaming Sunset'

Sub-variety of the magnificent, yellow-orange 'Mc Gredy's Sunset' but even more brightly colourful than the latter. It has many good qualities: very sound; strong, delicate scent, and pretty, shiny eaves.

207 Hybrid Tea Rose 'Mme. Caroline Testout'

Well-known, old-fashioned variety which should still be planted, as it is sound and unexacting, and particularly as it will tolerate some shade and even smoky city air. Sturdy in habit, flowers late and has a faint fragrance. The 'Arabella' variety carries its flowers better and is a purer pink, but is otherwise like 'Caroline Testout'.

208 Hybrid Tea Rose 'Mrs. Pierre S. Dupont'

Golden yellow, nicely shaped flowers and a good habit render this one of our best roses of the yellow group. Abundantly flowering and fragrant.

209 Hybrid Tea Rose 'Ophelia'

This variety will produce roses of good shape with particularly long stems especially if side buds are removed in time.

210 Floribunda 'Rose Alain'

For cultivation see No. 187. All the so called polyantha or floribunda rose will blossom abundantly, the flower growing in large umbels. They generally lack scent and are best used fo producing a massed effect in large borders, for which only one or two varieties which go well together should be chosen.

'Alain' is a very richly flowering variety with carmine-red flowers in large umbels; it will blossom for a long time and has a faint fragrance.

211 Floribunda Rose 'Frensham'

Variety of very sturdy habit and abundant blossom, needing a great amount of space; useful in front of shrubberies

212 Polyantha Pompon Rose 'Ellen Poulsen'

Sound, old-fashioned variety of low wide habit.

213 Floribunda Rose 'Julie Poulsen'

An unusual variety with single, large flowers in light umbels; reddish branches and leaves. It is especially lovely when cut.

214 Floribunda Rose 'Fashion'

One of the most fragrant in this group of delightful colour and beautiful shape in bud and flower alike.

215 Floribunda Rose 'Goldilocks'

Richly flowering, yellow variety of somewhat unusual colour. Luxuriant and sound.

216 Floribunda Rose 'Gruss an Aachen'

Does not resemble a real polyantha rose, but does belong to this group; will flower profusely, and is sound and luxuriant.

217 Floribunda Rose 'Irene of Denmark'

Enchanting small, white rose of very pretty habit and delightful green foliage.

218 Floribunda Rose 'Karen Poulsen'

Very clear, lasting, red colour and a charming rose for large clumps. Cultivation as for No. 210.

219 Floribunda Rose 'Margot Koster'

This lovely little rose is very useful for cutting.

220 Floribunda Rose 'Dick Koster'

Low, compact habit; good for cutting.

221 Floribunda Rose 'Orange Triumph'

Vigorous and wide variety with very glossy foliage and pretty, large umbels. Pretty colour, but so unusual that great care must be taken in using it together with other roses, or, indeed, any other flowers. For cultivation see No. 187.

222 Floribunda Rose 'Danish Gold'

Pretty, dwarf variety, which should be planted quite close together in order to produce the right effect.

223 Floribunda Rose 'Poulsen's Pink'

Luxuriant and tall of habit with pretty leaves; the flowers are rose-coloured with a faint yellow tinge. This variety will blossom abundantly. For cultivation, see No. 187.

224 Floribunda Rose 'Red Hat'

One of the most unexacting polyanthous roses that could be planted, as it will tolerate both some shade and city air. The bluish-red colour of the flowers makes it somewhat unsuited for mixing with other red varieties. For cultivation see No. 187.

225 Rambler Rose 'American Pillar'

This rose is a rambling or climbing type, although this name is somewhat misleading, as roses do not climb, but have to be trained to the wall or arbour. The varieties of vigorous habit with large umbels of fairly small, often non-fragrant flowers, should be pruned or thinned out every year or so, when some of the oldest stems should be cut off right down near the ground, and young rods should be trained up instead. The varieties with large flowers should be pruned in a slightly different way; the old rods should be left as long as they are fresh, and only part of the short side branches should be cut, as for dwarf roses with large flowers. The 'American Pillar' variety is a very vigorously growing rambler which may produce shoots of up to 10 ft in one summer and which, on the whole, needs plenty of space to develop well. It will blossom in June-July.

226 Rambler Rose 'Dorothy Perkins'

The flowers grow in very full, large bunches. It is fragrant, luxuriant and richly blossoming.

227 Rambler Rose 'Paul's Scarlet Climber'

This is surely the most-planted rambler to-day which is quite understandable, considering its wealth of flowers and good habit. However, care should be taken not to plant it against red walls and tiled roofs, where the red colour of the rose will take on an unattractive bluish tinge. Cultivation, as for No. 225. The 'Blaze' variety resembles the former closely, but will flower several times during the summer.

228 Rambler Rose 'Easlea's Golden Rambler'

Large, glowing, yellow flowers with faint fragrance and pretty leaves. Among other yellow varieties may be mentioned 'Carpet of Gold', richly flowering, but with small, charming, golden yellow flowers of delicate shape and delightful fragrance and 'Primavera', with dark yellow, well-formed, fragrant flowers.

229 Rambler Rose 'Excelsa'

One of the most abundantly flowering and luxuriant varieties, with small flowers. Cultivation as for No. 225.

230 Large-flowered Climbing Rose 'Gloire de Dijon'

This old-fashioned, well-known variety is still unsurpassed in certain respects. It may blossom against a wall facing south as early as the end of May, and will flower abundantly again several times in the course of the summer and far into the autumn. The lovely colour and very full flower, and the delicate tea-rose fragrance are all good reasons why it should still be planted in new gardens. Cultivation as for No. 225.

231 Rambler Rose 'Dr. W. Van Fleet'

A sound and luxuriant rose tree of very vigorous habit, and delightful, large, pink flowers. The variety 'New Dawn' resembles it exactly, but will blossom several times during the summer (perpetual). Cultivation as for No. 225.

232 Salix chrysocoma
Weeping Willow

Habitat: Europe, North Africa and Western Asia. Like poplars, willows are greedy plants, spreading their roots over a large area, and growing quickly. They should therefore be used cautiously in small gardens, but because of their unexacting nature and resistance to strong winds, they are well suited for sheltering zones in large country gardens. Because they are pretty and grow rapidly into large trees, they are planted too often in small gardens and the fact is overlooked that they may have a very unfortunate effect on other plants in one's own garden as well as one's neighbour's.

The tree will take severe pruning, but will lose its natural habit as a result. Planted near the edge of a lake, the weeping willow is of extra ordinary beauty.

233 Salix acutifolia
Violet Willow

Habitat: Russia, Siberia. Very accommodating variety thriving in dry, light soil as well as in damp boggy earth. One of the earliest willow trees to bloom, as its catkins may begin to burst into flower in the middle of mild winters. It will reach a height of 20-25 ft.

234 Salix viminalis
Common Osier

Habitat: Europe and Asia. Like the previous tree, handsome, early and copiously flowering 'pussy willow'. Useful for ordinary hedges and low uncut hedges in country gardens.

235 Salix caprea
Goat Willow or Great Sallow

Habitat: Europe and Eastern Asia. It has attractive, very large catkins, and is somewhat coarse and stiff in habit.

Among other handsome willow varieties may be mentioned *Salix purpurea* which grows into a lovely small tree or a large bush of 15-20 ft in height, and has pretty, dark-red branches in winter. A pendent variety of this willow, *Salix purpurea pendula*, is much better and more suitable in height for small gardens than the large, sturdy, weeping willow, No. 232.

236 Sambucus nigra
Common Elder

Habitat: Europe, North Africa and Western Asia. The elder is really one of our most delightful trees, full of poetry and gentle grace when flowering all over the country around midsummer, and delightful when bent under the weight of heavy, hanging, blue-black clusters of elder berry. The tree or bush will do best in deep, fertile soil, rich in humus, and not too dry; it will tolerate some shade, but will flower most abundantly in the sun. There are varieties with large, juicy fruits and others with charming, lobate leaves flecked with yellow. The elder, which is normally considered a tall bush, may grow into a pretty little tree of 15-20 ft.

237 Sambucus racemosa
Red Berried Elder

Habitat: Europe and Western Asia. Accommodating and shade-tolerating bush of 7-10 high. Good for planting among larger bushes. By itself in the open it will produce a great many yellow-green clusters of flowers early in April-May and, rarely, pretty, red clusters of berries in the autumn.

238 Sambucus canadensis
American Elderberry

It will produce very attractive, large, up to 2 ft wide racemes of flowers in August and small, black berries which are, however, inedible. By itself on a lawn or against a dark-coloured house, this giant-flowering elder will be of a most decorative effect. It will reach a height of about 10 ft and can be severely pruned at annual intervals.

239 Sorbaria arborea glabrata
Tree Spiraea

Habitat: China. This bush may reach a height of some 10 ft and planted by itself on a lawn or paved courtyard it will have a pretty habit with slightly pendent branches and long, pinnate leaves. The tips of the shoots will produce large, lacy, yellowish-white inflorescences about 1-2 ft in length in July-September. Thinning and cutting off old branches at annual intervals right down near the ground, together with slight trimming of the young ones, will produce larger and more luxuriant clusters of flowers.

240 Arundinaria nitida
Bamboo

Habitat: Central and Western China. These hardy bamboos should become fashionable, for they have a light and graceful effect if used with moderation. Planted among conifers and other evergreens or by themselves on a lawn, they will look smart, especially in conjunction with modern architecture. The soil should be deep humus, mixed with peat mould and must not be allowed to dry. Spring planting is best, and there must be no pruning until the plant is well established, when only dead shoots should be removed.

241 Sorbus aucuparia
Mountain Ash or Rowan

Habitat: Europe and Western Asia.

Observing how a rowan tree may grow spontaneously out of a crack in the wall of an old ruin, or in a crevice of a cliff with infinitesimal amounts of soil, it is easy to understand why this is considered one of the most unexacting and hardiest of our trees.

It is an excellent tree for a sheltering zone, in large shrubberies, or growing by itself in a front garden. It will reach a height of up to 23-26 ft, and may be planted either as a bush or as a tree with a tall trunk. There are varieties with particularly large red or orange-yellow fruits.

242　Sorbus intermedia
Swedish Whitebeam

Habitat: Northern Europe. This cannot compare with the mountain ash in beauty and handsome habit, but in the country will have a certain patient air, going well with grim surroundings, where the soil is poor and the wind strong. It is useful for high, wide, trimmed hedges in windy localities. The tree may reach some 35-50 ft in height.

243　Spiraea arguta
Bridal Wreath, Foam of May

All the tall spiraea varieties are among the best shrubs for small gardens, where they may form parts of groups or groups by themselves on lawns. Pruning should be limited to thinning out and cutting off old worn-out branches at annual intervals. They will thrive in ordinary, good garden soil; they tolerate some shade, but will flower profusely in the sun. They flower in April-May and reach 5-7 ft in height.

224　Spiraea bumalda
Anthony Waterer

This very righly flowering bush, of about 3 ft in height, is covered with rose-coloured and purple umbels of flowers in July-October, and is very

pretty as a hedge or bush planted in front of large clumps. It should be cut down completely every winter.

245　Spiraea vanhouttei

Hardy, unexacting and free flowering bush, well suited for planting in large groups in largish clumps. They may form large, isolated, sheltering hedges in the country, and will reach a height of about 8 ft. Pruning should be limited to thinning out old branches right down to the ground at annual intervals. Where there is room for an isolated spiraea on a lawn or among low bushes, the tall *Spiraea veitchii* may be recommended, whose 7-10 ft long, curving, elegant branches are full of clusters of flowers in July.

246　Stephanandra incisa

Habitat: Korea and Japan. A shrub with delicate reddish branches and small, charming, denticulated leaves, excellent for covering the ground between large bushes and trees, and useful on slopes. It will tolerate some shade, but does best in good soil; may reach a height of 4-8 ft and a still greater width. It may be cut down completely at annual intervals.

247　Symphoricarpos rivularis
Snowberry

Habitat: North America. Extraordinarily unexacting and shade-tolerant, but not especially attractive until the autumn, when the young branches are full of white, globular berries, charming against the wet earth. It is rewarding as an accommodating bush for filling in among large trees and shrubs, on the north side of hedges and tall houses, but will grow much better if allowed some sun and light. It produces suckers and should be thinned, constantly cutting out old worn-out branches. Height approximately 7 ft.

248 Symphoricarpos chenaultii
Hybrid Coral Berry

Small, shade-tolerant bush with delicate leaves and charming, rose-
coloured flowers and a wealth of red
and white berries at the tips of the
branches. It will grow about 5 ft tall.

249 Syringa chinensis
Rouen Lilac

The native country of this is France
where it was produced by crossing at
the end of the 18th century. It is a
delightful little bush of light, graceful,
but nevertheless rich habit; ideal for
groups in the small garden. It will
become laden with slightly pendent,
sweetly scented clusters at the end of
May and the first half of June. This
lilac is accommodating, and will grow
in fairly poor soil in exposed localities,
although it will become most beautiful
in good soil and in the warm air of a
garden walled in by hedges.
It grows 7-10 ft tall. There are also dark
purple and grayish-white varieties.

250 Syringa reflexa
Nodding Lilac

Habitat: China. With its long, pointed
inflorescences this does not resemble a
lilac, but is a pretty and strange, flowering bush of a height of up to 10-13
ft. It flowers in June.

251 Syringa tomentella
Downy Lilac

Habitat: China. The light, slender
inflorescences cover the whole bush
with a veil of dark-rose, fragrant flowers in June. It does best in ordinary
soil in full sunlight.

252 Syringa vulgaris 'Souvenir de Louis Spaeth',
Lilac

All the improved forms of *Syringa
vulgaris* are undoubtedly the prettiest
shrubs of the garden, and the gardens
which do not possess a lilac are easily
counted; and we all look forward to
the time when the lilac will blossom
among laburnums and red may in the
quiet, suburban lanes. Great improve-
ments have now occured in this species
of plants, so that we need no longer be
content with our grandparents' charming, small-flowering lilacs. Some of
the best in each group of colour will be
mentioned below.
In addition to this variety, the dark
purple, single flower 'Vulcan' and
the double, mauve 'Katherine Have-
meyer' with very large clusters, may be
recommended; other colours are mentioned under the next two varieties.
Lilacs will do best in ordinary loam,
which must not be too wet or cold.
They may be used among other and
lower bushes, but are often loveliest on
their own on a lawn in full sunlight.
Pruning consists of moderate cutting-
back just after flowering at annual
intervals, or of a strong rejuvenating
process, if the bush has grown scraggy
and thin. Ground shoots forming 'wild'
lilacs should be removed by scraping
away the earth around the bush a
little, and cutting off the wild shoots
with a sharp knife close to the root.
Lilacs may grow very tall, up to 13-16 ft.

253 Syringa vulgaris 'Mme Lemoine'
Lilac

Old-fashioned, pretty and vigorous,
double variety, white in colour.
Among other white ones, the double,
greenish-white, early-blossoming 'Princess Clementine' is very pretty.

254 Syringa vulgaris 'Michel Buchner'
Lilac

Very long, light mauve, very full inflorescences, which turn rose-coloured
when fully out.

The 'Mons. Leon Mathieu' variety is of wide, good habit and very richly blossoming with light mauve, single-flower clusters.

255 Tamarix pentandra
Tamarisk

Habitat: Southern Europe and Western Asia. This elegant shrub, with delicate leaves and large, heather-like inflorescences appearing in August-September, does best in full sunlight and light soil. Should be cut back severely after planting, but otherwise no pruning. It can be grown by itself or among low bushes. Height 10-13 ft.
Another vigorously-growing variety is *Tamarix parviflora*, which flowers in April-May.

256 Tilia platyphyllos
Broad-leaved Lime

Habitat: Europe. This handsome park tree which, in the past, was used for long avenues in manor house and large country gardens, is somewhat too large and shady for ordinary gardens. On the other hand, the lime tree may be used for high hedges in good growing conditions, i.e. soil rich in humus and not too windy a locality. For this purpose the small-leafed linden, *Tilia cordata*, would be best.
The lime tree may grow up to 65 ft in height.

257 Ulmus glabra
Wych or Scotch Elm

Habitat: Europe and Western Asia. The elm should never be used in an ordinary garden, as it is very greedy, grows far too large and, as a result of its intense fruitfulness, will give lawns, etc., a faded and autumnal look when the seeds are falling. As a tree of character in the sheltering hedge of a country garden it will look attractive; it is very accommodating. The variety *Ulmus carpinifolia*, small-leafed elm, is useful for tall, sheltering hedges. The elm may reach a height of 85 ft.

258 Viburnum carlesii

Habitat: Korea. In this family we find some of the most fragrant shrubs, and when in flower in April-May, the charming white umbels of flowers, pink in bud, spread a fragrance like that of a hundred lilies-of-the valley. It does best in deep soil, rich in humus, in light localities, but not where there is burning sunshine all day. No pruning is necessary, as it is nearly always grafted, attention should be paid to the shoots from the root, which must be removed as soon as possible. Grows approximately 4 ft high. The hybrid *Viburnum burkwoodii* is evergreen and a little taller of habit.

259 Viburum farreri (fragrans)

Habitat: Northern China. As early as December, this bush may begin to flower if the weather is mild; very strongly scented. Cultivation as for No. 258.

260 Viburnum lantana
Wayfaring Tree

Habitat: Europe and Western Asia. This bush has a fairly coarse and robust habit, with thick, grey, matted leaves, large greyish-white inflorescences in June and pretty black and red berries in late summer. It is very hardy, will tolerate poor soil and strong winds, and is excellent as a sheltering hedge. Height, some 13-16 ft.

261 Viburnum opulus sterile
Snowball Tree

Habitat: Europe, Western Asia and North Africa. Unexacting and wind resistant bush which, planted alone on a lawn, looks delightful in June when bent under all its white snowball flowers. It may grow up to 10 ft high.

262 Viburnum rhytidophyllum

Habitat: Central China. In localities in half-shade, e.g. against a wall facing north or east, this shrub will be very lovely, growing long, most peculiar, leathery, wrinkled, evergreen leaves, which look very pretty against a brick wall. It will attain 7-10 ft in height.

263 Viscum album
Misletoe

This strange, parasitic bush, well-known for its use at Christmas, may grow on several species of trees, but does best on apple-trees, mountain ash and may; the variety growing best on apple trees should preferably be "sown" again on an appletree. The dissemination of seeds is done by birds in Nature, but can also be done by taking fresh, ripe, hibernated seeds from an old mistletoe about May and rubbing them on fairly young branches of an appletree. The sticky berries will cling to branches, and after a year or two the first small misletoe plant will appear. As there are both male and female plants, a quantity of seeds should be sown if it is desired to obtain fruits from the new plants.

264 Vinca major
Greater Periwinkle

Habitat: Europe and Asia Minor. This creeping evergreen is one of the prettiest and most suitable plants for covering the ground among bushes and trees. It will become prettiest and most vigorous if the soil is not too dry or heavy. The *Vinca minor* mentioned below is the better of the two varieties, and both will flower prettily in April-May. Five to eight plants per square

yard will produce good, compact cover in the course of only a few years.

265 Vinca minor
Lesser Periwinkle

Habitat: Europe, Western Asia. Uses as for No. 264. It will also form attractive borders around large rose beds.

266 Vinca major variegata
Variegated Greater Periwinkle

Uses as for No. 264, although it needs a somewhat lighter locality to become prettily flecked with yellow.

267 Weigela 'Abel Carriere'

Very attractive, richly blossoming garden bush. It is wide and slightly pendent of habit, so that it should preferably be planted in front of a clump or in groups, isolated on a lawn. It will do best in deep, fresh, fertile humus, and in the sun. At intervals of a few years the bush should be rejuvenated by cutting out old, worn-out branches level with the ground. It will grow some 7 ft tall and equally wide, and flowers in June-July.

268 Weigela 'Mont Blanc'

Uses and cultivation as for No. 267.

269 Weigela 'Le Printemps'

On of the smallest dwarf varieties. Uses and cultivation as for No. 267.

270 Weigela hybrida 'Styriaca'

Flowering abundantly, of medium height. In addition, there are the following good varieties: 'Eduard Andre', of medium height and dark red; 'Saturne', low, early and a glowing red; *Weigela middendorffiana*, low in habit, early and with sulphur yellow flowers. Uses and instructions as for cultivation No. 267.

II CLIMBERS

Under this common denominator, all the tree-like plants have been collected, which either climb or creep up walls or arbour pillars, etc., spontaneously, or are of a markedly climbing or creeping habit, so that they must be trained, and thus serve decorative purposes in the garden.

Climbing roses, or 'ramblers', as they are more commonly called, are illustrated immediately after ordinary roses and described under Nos. 225-31.

271 Acitinidia kolomikta

Habitat: Eastern Asia. Climbing bush, hooking itself to arbours or poles by the petioles, which grows best in a sheltered spot and in porous soil, rich in humus. It may climb up to a height of 16 ft.

272 Aristolochia macrophylla
Dutchman's Pipe

Habitat: Eastern North America. The very large, fresh, green leaves give the plant a pretty and decorative look, if planted against a wall or an arbour post. It is so characteristic and dominant in appearance that other, more slender climbers should not be planted near it. The small, insignificant flowers behind the large leaves are very amusing in shape. It does well in half-shade and in sunlight alike.

273 Celastrus scandens
Staff Tree

Habitat: North America. One common name of this plant 'Tree killer' is due to the unpleasant habit of this vigorously growing climber of overgrowing and strangling old trees in the wild. In a garden it will look attractive on an archway or against a wall; it is accommodating with regard to soil, etc. Its beauty comes mainly from the large seed vessels with shining red and yellow fruits. As some forms are unisexual, care must be taken to obtain bisexual stock, otherwise there will not be any fruit.

274 Campsis radicans
Trumpet Vine

Habitat: North America. Although this pretty, self-clinging climber is not hardy in very cold districts, an attempt should be made to plant it where a sheltered, warm position is available against a wall facing south.

275 Clematis montana rubens
Mountain Clematis

Habitat: China, Himalaya. The clematis family, with its many species and large-flowering varieties, and in all its variations, is the prettiest type of climber we can use in the garden. On a wall facing south or a light wall facing north, against a fir hedge or an arbour, or simply growing wild around an old, gnarled branch stuck into the lawn, wherever it is grown, clematis will add beauty to the garden with its light, graceful habit and wealth of colourful flowers from the hanging vines. Clematis does not like a scorching hot locality with dry, stiff soil. The soil should be deep, leaf-mould rich in humus, and must not dry out, so that there should always be a thin layer of half-decayed leaves or old dung on the soil around the plant.

It blossoms in May-June and needs no pruning, nor too much training, as long, freely hanging vines will produce the greatest amount of blossom and look most graceful. It may grow to an imposing height, up to 33 ft.

276 Clematis 'Comtesse de Bouchaud'

Sound and vigorous variety, flowering in July-August.

277 Clematis jackmanii

Probably the most frequently planted, large-flowering variety, blossoming abundantly and for a long period from July to September.

278 Clematis 'The President'

The large flowers are of an unusually pure, deep blue colour and come in June-July.

279 Clematis 'Lasurstern'

It has very large flowers in June-July, and is the soundest and most vigorous of all the varieties.

280 Clematis 'Nelly Moser'

This has enormous flowers of fragile beauty, and may flower as early as the end of May.

281 Clematis tangutica
Mongolian Clematis

Habitat: Mongolia. The strangely shaped, yellow flowers and the delicate, silky seed vessels give this variety a beauty which the others do not possess. It does not produce very long growths, and flowers in June-July.

282 Clematis vitalba
Traveller's Joy

If it is desired to cover an ugly old paling or wall as quickly as possible, this is one of the best plants to grow on account of its unusually vigorous growth. It is accommodating and does not mind shade.

283 Clematis viticella kermesina

Habitat: Southern Italy. It is very hardy and accommodating, with fairly small, but charming flowers in late summer.

284 Hedera helix
Common Ivy

Habitat: Europe. A delightful, self-clinging, evergreen plant for covering ugly wall surfaces and palings, and for creating a quiet, evergreen carpet among shrubs and trees. It will cling best to brick walls and coarse concrete walls. It grows well in the shade, and in humus-rich, not too dry, soil. Once a year, old ivy growing up walls should be trimmed, i.e. on old creepers all leaves and long shoots should be closely cut in the month of April.
The small-leafed and other varieties of the ivy are more compact and attractive, but slower in growth than No. 286.

285 Hedera helix arborescens
Tree Ivy

When the common, climbing ivy grows older, it will start flowering, and fruiting and the flowering branches will have leaves of a different shape and no clinging roots. They may be propagated by cuttings, producing a bush-like ivy which is pretty and shade-tolerant.

286 Hedera helix hibernica
Irish Ivy

Large-leafed variety of common ivy, but more vigorous in growth than the latter. Cultivation as for No. 284.

287 Hedera colchica
Persian Ivy

Very large leaves of a shape different from that of common ivy. See No. 284.

288 Hydrangea petiolaris
Climbing Hydrangea

Habitat: Japan. Peculiar, climbing bush, which can cling to coarse walls and tree trunks with its own aerial roots, like ivy. It will flower prettily in sunny localities, but will also tolerate some shade.

289 Jasminum nudiflorum
Winter Jasmine

Habitat: China. This elegant shrub with green branches needs training as it cannot climb or cling upwards on its own. As early as before Christmas, the graceful, primula-like flowers will appear, delightfully brightening the garden. It should be planted somewhere against the wall of the house, where it can be seen from the sitting-room, preferably against a warm wall facing south-west. The old parts of the branches should be pruned a little every year just after flowering, allowing for constant growth of new, young branches.

290 Lonicera heckrottii
Honeysuckle

The honeysuckle is a well-known old favourite among the creepers, mainly because of its delightful fragrance. There are many varieties more beautiful than the common woodbine, No. 291, but they all like a shady spot and slightly damp humus. *Lonicera heckrottii* is a hybrid and somewhat slow in growth, but has pretty foliage and unusual eaves.

291 Lonicera caprifolium
Perfoliate Honeysuckle

Habitat: Europe and Western Asia. This honeysuckle and the common woodbine, *Lonicera periclymenum*, are very charming and easily grown, and will blossom from June to August.

292 Lonicera henryi
Honeysuckle

Habitat: Western China. An evergreen charming variety of honeysuckle which looks pretty against a wall facing north as a change from common ivy.

293 Lonicera tellmanniana
Honeysuckle

A vigorously growing and abundantly flowering hybrid between *L. trago-phylla*, and *L. sempervirens* blossoming in June. The species, *Lonicera trago-phylla* has bright orange-yellow clusters of flowers in June-July and is one of the prettiest honeysuckles known, but lacks fragrance.

294 Parthenocissus tricuspidata
Boston Ivy

Habitat: China and Japan The very widely used, self-clinging Boston Ivy may cover large areas of wall surface in a few years. It will cling best to brick and concrete walls, but does not cling very well to whitewashed surfaces. It will thrive in ordinary good soil, and in sunlight as well as in half-shade.
The variety, *Parthenocissus tricuspidata Lowii*, is not quite so vigorous in habit and has somewhat smaller leaves; both will take on very pretty hues in the autumn.

295 Parthenocissus quinquefolia
Virginia Creeper

Habitat: North America, Pretty, self-clinging Virginia creeper with attractive autumn colours.
Parthenocissus inserta closely resembles this species but is not self-clinging, can be used for covering trellis and similar purposes. It is wise to cut back the long shoots a little each winter.

296 Polygonum baldschuanicum
Russian Vine

Habitat: Turkestan. Possibly the most vigorous in habit among creepers, it should be planted only where there is plenty of space and where it cannot suffocate other plants. In a dry, sunny locality it will flower profusely in July-September.

297 Wisteria sinensis
Chinese Wisteria

Habitat: China. When the wisteria's long, graceful clusters of flowers are suspended among the tender, reddish young foliage in May-June, we all marvel at its great beauty. If it is made to flower on an arbour, mirrored in a small lake or pond, it will look more than twice as enchanting.

Otherwise, this plant likes a warm, sunny locality in porous, calcareous, fresh loam, and if it grows very vigorously the strongest side branches may be pruned every year in August. It will then form short, somewhat gnarled spurs as in fruit trees.

298 Vitis vinifera
Grape Vine

Habitat: Europe, North Africa and Western Asia. Planted against a wall facing south in good, porous, calcareous and nourishing soil, a so-called

"outdoor vine" may produce pretty, green leaves and vines, as well as quite nice bunches of grapes. Pruning must be undertaken no later than January, all thin shoots being trimmed to firm side buds, whereupon the thick, long rods should be trained to the wall or trellis. In summer, the side shoots are pinched off a few leaves above the rudimentary bunches of grapes. The variety, 'Precose de Malingre', is the safest for ripening out-of-doors, but in warm summers such varieties as 'Chasselas Tokay Rose' may ripen well and bear larger, greenish-red grapes.

299 Vitis vinifera 'Precose de Malingre'
Grape Vine

Cultivation as for No. 298.

300 Vitis vinifera 'Burgundy Blue'
Grape Vine

Cultivation as for No. 298.

III CONIFERS

This group of trees and bushes have certain botanical characteristics in common, e.g. needle-shaped leaves, seeds in cones and flowers without petals. They are generally evergreens, but one or two among them will shed their leaves in winter.

301 Abies concolor
Colorado White Fir

Habitat: North America. A stately, handsome fir, reaching some 50 ft in height. It does well in ordinary good soil, but will not develop so well in the shade, or tolerate city air very well.

302 Abies homolepis
Nikko Fir

Habitat: Japan. A compact, attractive, dark green, silver fir which may reach a height of some 40-50 ft in good garden soil in an open locality.

303 Abies cephalonica
Grecian Fir

Habitat: Greece. Like the foregoing

two varieties, this handsome fir should be planted only where there is plenty of space in which to develop, i.e. on a large lawn or among low, creeping bushes. It will grow up to 40-50 ft in height.

304 Abies procera glauca
Blue Noble Fir

Habitat: North America. One of the most attractive, so-called 'blue firs', which under good conditions, i.e. sheltered from strong winds and in good, fresh, porous soil and with room to develop, will become extremely handsome. If varieties of bent, picturesque habit are preferred, these can generally be obtained and, used with discrimination, may look magnificent in a large rockery, especially as they are full of purple inflorescences in the spring, followed by large, vertically placed cones.

305 Abies pinsapo
Spanish Fir

Habitat: Spain. Erect growing and up to 35 ft tall, or as a crooked, picturesque, spreading variety, this is a handsome tree.

306 Abies alba
European Silver Fir

Habitat: Central Europe. The common silver fir may be used as a temporray shelter for other, better varieties of silver, fir, and for planting among evergreen trees on the whole. It will tolerate some shade.

307 Cedrus deodara
Deodar

Habitat: Himalaya. Cedar trees are very attractive and characteristic conifers but unfortunately not quite hardy enough for very cold areas. Planted where there is good shelter, deep humus and plenty of space, specimens of up to 200 ft may develop. A cover on the ground, consisting of peat mould, leaf mould, bracken, and other very low ground plants will undoubtedly increase the resistance of these trees to cold. They should always be planted in such a way as to ensure that neighbouring trees or large bushes cannot trouble them.

308 Cedrus atlantica glauca
Blue Cedar

Habitat: Atlas Mountains. With its silver-blue bundles of needles on the sloping, slightly pendent branches, this is a very attractive and strange tree, and three to five specimens, planted close together, will eventually form an unusually imposing group on a lawn. From the Bible we know the cedars of Lebanon, *Cedrus libani*; magnificent, large specimens of which are to be found in English manor house gardens and a few are still growing in their wild state in Asia Minor.

309 Chamaecyparis lawsoniana
Lawson Cypress

Habitat: North America. The Lawson cypress is a species extremely rich in varieties, with all sorts of habit, from slender pillar or columnar shapes to quite pendulous, spreading and dwarf types; the colour of the needles may also vary from fresh green to silver green and almost pure yellow.

It does best in not too calcareous, humus-rich soil in full light and well sheltered. Several can be planted together, as handsome evergreen groups near the entrance of the house, or in other places in the garden; they may also be mixed with other conifers but will not look their best in conjunction with deciduous bushes. The most characteristic varieties with pendant or pillar-shaped habits will look most attractive planted by themselves on a lawn. Among the many varieties of *Chamaecyparis lawsoniana*, all of which will grow fairly tall. up to 35 ft, may be mentioned 'Chamaecyparis Triomphe de Boskoop', a very charming variety of loose habit and arching branchlets. Glaucous blue.

310 Chamaecyparis lawsoniana allumii
Lawson Cypress

Of wide, pyramidal habit and with blue-green needles.

311 Chamaecyparis lawsoniana wisselii
Lawson Cypress

Of slender habit with curly, moss-like

branches, which render this variety rather unusual.

312 Chamaecyparis nootkatensis
Nootka Cypress

Habitat: North America. An undemanding variety which may do well in some shade and in city gardens.

The variety, *Chamaecyparis nootkatensis glauca*, which is not much grown, is very strange looking and of vigorous, pendant habit. Cultivation as for No. 309.

313 Chamaecyparis nootkatensis pendula
Weeping Nootka Cypress

Unusually pendent habit, branches almost trailing along the ground. Cultivation as for No. 309.

314 Chamaecyparis obtusa
Hinoki Cypress

Habitat: Japan. A handsome, unexpecting variety of a fresh, green colour; may be used as No. 309. It will reach 50 ft in height, but there are varieties of less vigorous habit as well.

315 Chamaecyparis obtusa nana
Dwarf Hinoki Cypress

Very dwarf variety, only 2-3 ft high, charming for a rockery or among other dwarf conifers. Cultivation as for No. 309.

316 Chamaecyparis pisifera plumosa
Sawara Cypress

Habitat: Japan. Hardy and attractive variety of pyramidal habit and pretty, curly branches. Cultivation as for No. 309.

317 Chamaecyparis pisifera filifera
Slender Sawara Cypress

Habitat: Japan. A relative of the fore-going tree, with broad, pretty, pendulous habit.

318 Chamaecyparis pisifera squarrosa
Sawara Cypress

Habitat: Japan. Irregular habit and attractive, silver blue colour. Cultivation as for No. 309. In addition, there is a handsome, yellowish-green variety, *Chamaecyparis pisifera squarrosa sulphurea* which, like the original species, *Chamaecyparis pisifera*, is of vigorous, erect habit with slightly overhanging shoot tips.

319 Cryptomeria japonica lobbii
Lobb's Japanese Cedar

Habitat: Japan. A tall (up to 35-50 ft) slender conifer with dense erect branches and pyramidal habit. Unfortunately it prefers the mildest and moistest districts. It will tolerate pruning as opposed to several other conifers. It should be planted in a moist, spacious locality in light, humus-rich soil with a limited content of lime, given plenty of room and sheltered from strong winds.

320 Cryptomeria japonica elegans
Japanese Cedar

A low, bushy variety with very delicate branches, turning completely bronze-coloured in winter.

321 Juniperus media pfitzeriana
Pfitzer Juniper

Habitat: Eastern Asia. *J. media* and its varieties are evergreens which are widely grown in gardens, for nearly every purpose. Besides being easily grown and handsome, this form may be strongly recommended for such desired purposes as covering a terraced slope or as single plants in a rockery, etc.

Juniperus media pfitzeriana will grow into a very broad bush (up to 10 ft) with long, elegant, overhanging branches. Its colour is a bluish-green, but there is a variety with pretty, yellow tips.

322 Juniperus chinensis pyramidalis
Chinese Juniper

Habitat: Asia Minor. Wide, pillar-like habit and blue-grey colour. It may reach a height of up to 10-13 ft.

323 Juniperus communis suecica
Swedish Juniper

Habitat: Europe and Western America. This Scandinavian juniper of pillar-like habit may grow some 7-10 ft tall and is very decorative among dwarf varieties of juniper and heather. It will do best in light soil and full sunlight.

324 Juniperus horizontalis
Creeping Juniper

Habitat: North America. For covering the ground among other tall junipers and for planting along the plinth of a house, or for placing in a rockery, this dwarf creeping juniper is excellent. One plant may cover more than 4 square feet, but two plants per square foot should be suitable.

325 Juniperus chinensis japonica
Dwarf Chinese Juniper

Habitat: China. Pretty, spreading habit and yellowish needles.

326 Juniperus sabina tamarisci-folia
Tamarisk Savin

Habitat: Southern Europe. Caucasus and Siberia. The most handsome type among the low, compact junipers; its colour is a fresh, deep green. It is most useful among other junipers and in rockeries.

327 Juniperus squamata meyeri
Meyer's Juniper

Habitat: China and Himalaya. Very pretty, blue-green colour and not very vigorous in habit. It grows up to 3-5 f in height and may be shaped by carefu pruning and training.

328 Juniperus virginiana glauca
Pencil Juniper

Habitat: Eastern North America. Fairly tall juniper of slender although irregular, picturesque habit and a delightfu blue-grey colour. It may eventuall grow about 15-20 ft tall or more. Ver attractive, planted together with type such as Nos. 327 and 326, as thei bluish-green hues look well togethe

329 Larix decidua
Common Larch

Habitat: Europe. This graceful, ligh forest tree could be used in garden planted together with pine, fir, junipe and other conifers, but must have plen ty of space, and will develop best in a open locality. Needs light, porous soi not too wet in winter. It may reach height of some 100 ft.

330 Larix kaempferi (leptolepis)
Japanese Larch

Habitat: Japan. A sound and rapidl growing species, handsome in winte with the reddish-brown bark of it boughs. It may reach 50-65 ft in heigh

331 Picea glauca
White Spruce

Habitat: North America. One of th most accommodating and wind resis tant of the firs, and much better fo sheltering zones, etc., than Norwa spruce. Like other firs, it does not lik shade and smoky city air, however. I it is desired to use fir for a high, wid hedge, silver fir should be preferre (in very exposed situations, the Sitk spruce, No. 336, may also be used), as it will take quite severe trimming. It will reach a height of up to 35 ft.

332 Picea abies
Norway Spruce, Christmas Tree

Habitat: Northern and Central Europe. The popular Christmas tree can be grown as a garden tree, if planted in light, porous soil, given sun and some shelter, but it is not always the best fir to choose.

There are many varieties, from the dwarf *Picea abies pygmaea* and *Picea abies procumbens* to tall, erect species such as *Picea abies pyramidata* and peculiar, almost abnormal varieties with snake-like branches, e.g. *Picea abies virgata*. If these varieties are used in the right manner, i.e. the dwarf varieties for the rockery and the tall varieties on a lawn by themselves, they could all be used in an ordinary garden.

333 Picea glauca conica
Dwarf White Spruce

Charming, very dwarf variety of silver fir which, surrounded by very low, carpet-forming rock plants such as Thymus, Saxifraga, etc. will look attractive in a rockery. It may reach a height of about 3 ft.

334 Picea pungens glauca
Blue Spruce

Habitat: North America. Very accommodating and wind-tolerant, and when older, of stately, straight, slightly stiff habit. The variety *Picea pungens argentea* takes on a pretty silver-blue hue; such 'silver firs' are greatly coveted by many garden owners, although they must be planted with discretion owing to their cold appearance. Young plants will often grow crooked and unattractive in habit; for this reason the top shoot should be trained to a stake during the first few years.

335 Picea omorica
Serbian Spruce

Habitat: The Balkan Peninsula. Undoubtedly the most attractive in shape and habit among the firs, slender and tall like a church spire and with slightly swaying branches and pendent side boughs. It will gradually begin to resemble a stately pagoda, tracing its dark green profile against the evening sky. It will thrive in any soil and tolerates city air better than other firs, but should nevertheless be planted in an isolated group of three to seven specimens on a lawn, or else only very low bushes should be planted around it. It may reach a height of 50-100 ft.

336 Picea sitchensis
Sitka Spruce

Habitat: North America. Very vigorous in habit, and hardy with unpleasantly prickly needles, occasionally earning for it the nickname of 'Thistle Fir'. This fir is excellent for a sheltering zone around a country house in exposed surroundings; it will tolerate hedge trimming may grow 80-100 ft. high.

337 Pinus cembra
Arolla Pine

Habitat: Siberia and the Alps. In general, the pine is a very unexacting tree as far as soil is concerned, and will as a rule grow more handsomely in poor, porous, gravelly soil than in too nourishing, damp soil, rich in humus. The pine will develop best in light and sun, and does not tolerate shade from the overhanging branches of other trees. The soil around the plant should be kept loose in the first few years, but should not be deeply dug with a spade; later, decayed needles, etc. should be allowed to cover the earth in peace; many acid-soil plants (e.g. Rhododendrons) will thrive excellently beneath such old pines with high trunks. The less vigorous varieties will look attractive on the lawn, near the house, or in a front garden where they will form a nice contrast to the house both in summer and in winter. The pine does not tolerate pruning, but if planted as a wide hedge around a terrace it would be wise to pinch off the central top shoot in the spring while soft (especially on *Pinus mugo*, No. 339). The Arolla pine is of fairly slender and moderate habit, and one of the best varieties of pine for ordinary gardens. It may reach a height of 100 ft.

338 Pinus contorta
Beach Pine

Habitat: North America. Often a low, bushy pine, useful for compact, sheltering hedges in exposed localities. It will reach 30-200 ft in height.

339 Pinus mugo
Mountain Pine

Habitat: Central Europe. Of low habit and broader than No. 338. *Pinus mugo mughus* has a dwarf habit.

340 Pinus nigra
Austrian Pine

Habitat: Southern Europe. Its habit is broad and vigorous and the long needles are of a delightful, dark green colour, giving this pine a sound and luxuriant look all the year round. It tolerates wind and poor soil, and will grow most attractive in a light, sunny locality, but needs plenty of space in order to unfold in all its glory. May grow up to 80 ft tall.

341 Pinus parviflora
Japanse White Pine

Habitat: Japan. Along with the Arolla pine, this variety is undoubtedly one of the best varieties of pine for planting in an ordinary garden. It is of broad, uneven, picturesque habit and over the

years will produce a great many pretty cones. It reaches 25-50 ft. in height.

342 Pinus peuce
Macedonian Pine

Habitat: The Balkans. Resembles the Arolla pine, No. 337, in many ways, but is taller and more open in habit.

343 Pinus silvestris
Scots Pine

Habitat: Europe. Very accommodating and wind-tolerant pine which, however will soon grow thin and ugly in gardens if squeezed among other trees and large bushes. It grows best in sandy soil and may attain 100 ft. in height.

344 Pinus strobus
Weymouth Pine

Habitat: North America. Vigorously growing, tall variety of pine with very pretty, long, soft bunches of needles and long, decorative cones. It may reach a height of 80-100 ft.

345 Pseudotsuga menziesii
Oregon Douglas Fir

Habitat: Western North America. Grows very rapidly, but will, unfortunately soon grow too large for an ordinary garden. It may reach a height of more than 300 ft. The variety, *Pseudotsuga menziesii viridis*, of the coast regions is called 'palm-tree fir' and has very pretty, dark green shiny needles especially useful for cutting for ornamental purposes.

346 Sciadopitys verticillata
Umbrella Pine

Habitat: Japan. Its name alludes to the needles on the young shoots which are like the ribs of an umbrella. The habit of the plant is erect and like a narrow pyramid. Among other evergreens a few specimens would look nice. The tree or bush is slow in growth and will reach a height of some 50 ft. It grows best in good soil, rich in humus, and with good shelter.

347 Sequoiadendron giganteum
Wellingtonia

Habitat: California. This tree which, in its native country, grows in the Sierra Nevada, for more than 2,000 years has formed incredibly large trees of more than 350 ft in height, and with trunks so thick that cars can drive through holes hewn out of them at the base. Specimens of 150 ft. in height may be found in the English gardens. It will do best in porous, humus rich soil, which must not be too dry.

348 Taxodium distichum
Swamp Cypress

Habitat: North America. This deciduous conifer will produce graceful, new growth in late spring, developing into brackenlike foliage of the lightest and palest green. Near a lake or bog it will send up strange aerial roots or 'knees' from the base. It will also grow in ordinary garden soil in a sheltered garden, and may reach up to 100 ft. in height.

349 Taxus baccata
Common or English Yew

Habitat: Europe. Very attractive and shade-tolerant, wide bush or small tree, particularly well suited for city gardens as a background for low, flowering shrubs or herbaceous borders. It can also be used for broad hedges or for trimming into massive shapes, contrasting with the freely-growing bushes of the garden. In deep soil, rich in humus and covered with peat mould, old leaves or old dung, it will grow pretty and luxuriant in habit. The yew may each 60 ft. in height.

The *Taxus cuspidata*, Japanese Yew is

hardier, and of lighter and more open habit than *Taxus baccata*.

350 Taxus baccata fastigiata
Irish Yew

Slender, compact, pillar-like habit and often used in churchyards, but will also form lovely hedges. A handsome, pendulous variety is called *Taxus baccata dovastoniana*

351 Taxus baccata aurea
Golden Yew

Yellow shoot tips, attractive-looking especially in the spring.

352 Thuja occidentalis
American Arbor-vitae

Habitat: North America. Many garden owners dislike thuja for its unpleasant smell and somewhat dreary aspect. If a dark corner of the garden or an ugly wall surface needs to be covered, the arbor vitae will, however, be useful. It will also quickly form high hedges around the garden in good soil conditions (noncalcareous soil), *Thuja occidentalis fastigiata*, of compact, pillar-like habit being best suited for this purpose.

353 Thuja plicata
Western Red Cedar

Habitat: North America. Very accommodating and hardy thuja, useful as a sheltering plant for other, more delicate conifers. It grow 100 ft or more in height.

354 Thuja standishii
Japanese Arbor-vitae

Habitat: China and Japan. This plant is very handsome, with broad, pendulous branchlets. Planted on a lawn on its own, it will look most attractive after a few years, and will not resemble an ordinary thuja at all. It will reach a height of 30-50 ft.

355 Thujopsis dolobrata
Hiba

Habitat: Japan. The peculiar, sturdy, scale-like needles which give the plant a stiff and somewhat cold look. Accommodating both as regards soil and light, it will even thrive on the north side of a house and in back gardens, where it may develop into a broad bush of some 13-16 ft in height. *Thujopsis dolobrata nana* is an attractive, palegreen variety, useful for planting among evergreens.

356 Tsuga heterophylla
Western Hemlock

Habitat: North-Western America. Of light, uneven habit, but its straight pyramid shape resembles that of a fir. It will do best in non-calcareous, deep soil, rich in humus, which must not be allowed to dry out; must be sheltered from strong winds. A delicate, graceful tree if planted by itself, or a few specimens may look well grown together in a light, but sheltered corner of the lawn. It may reach a height of some 65 ft or more.

357 Tsuga canadensis
Eastern Hemlock

Habitat: North America. This is wider and more uneven in habit than the previous variety, and will reach up to 100 ft. in height. A less vigorous variety, *Tsuga diversifolia*, may be used for small gardens. It is of slightly pendulous habit, hardy and will tolerate some shade.

INDEX OF LATIN NAMES

References are to page numbers

INDEX OF ENGLISH NAMES

References are to page numbers

PLANTS THAT FEED AND SERVE US
by Else Hvass
English Editor: E.B. Anderson

'Ideal examples of what good Natural History books should be, containing coloured illustrations whose clarity is second to none and whose accuracy and attention to detail shows that the artist is thoroughly conversant with the subject. Indeed it is visual identification that is the criterion of these handy volumes.'   *School Government Chronicle*

MUSHROOMS AND TOADSTOOLS IN COLOUR
by Else and Hans Hvass

'Pocket book with 343 accurately drawn fungi in full colour. First-rate drawings and descriptions.'   *Country Life*

DOGS OF THE WORLD
by Ivan Swedrup,
English Editor: Rosamund Oldfield

'A work of great skill and love, listing with concise notes and depicting in lively, well-coloured paintings 146 breeds of dogs from all over the world, including the 106 breeds recognised by the Kennel Club.'
Gamekeeper and Countryside

INSECTS IN COLOUR
Edited by N.D. Riley

267 species clearly illustrated and described, with notes on habits and occurrence.

POND AND STREAM LIFE
Edited by John Clegg

369 species illustrated and clearly described.

WOODLAND LIFE IN COLOUR
by G. Mandahl-Barth
Edited by Arnold Darlington

686 species, including all the commoner invertebrate animals which live in woods, hedgerows and timbered gardens, illustrated in full colour, with descriptive notes.

FIELD AND MEADOW LIFE IN COLOUR
by L. Lyneborg
Edited by Arnold Darlington

621 species, covering all forms of lower fauna from worms, woodlice and centipedes to insects, spiders and slugs. Full descriptive text.

SEASHORE LIFE IN COLOUR
by Gwynne Vevers

64 pages of coloured illustrations of 263 creatures and plants found on the seashore, with descriptions.

POISONOUS PLANTS IN COLOUR
by Pamela North

Prepared in co-operation with the Pharmaceutical Society of Great Britain. Helps the recognition of plants and fungi which could be poisonous.

PLANT GALLS IN COLOUR
by Arnold Darlington

A representative selection, with 80 pages of coloured illustrations.

MOUNTAIN FLOWERS IN COLOUR
by Anthony Huxley

A unique pocket guide, giving a comprehensive coverage of European mountain flowers. 1200 plants illustrated, 884 in full colour

POCKET ENCYCLOPAEDIA OF WILD FLOWERS IN COLOUR
by H. Skytte Christiansen

557 full colour illustrations with full descriptions and details of where they may be found.

PEOPLES OF THE WORLD IN COLOUR
by Francis Huxley

A colourful panorama of Mankind, presenting many tribes and races, with 321 coloured illustrations arranged in six main sections.
Every spread is attractively arranged, and there are maps showing where the peoples live. Mr. Francis Huxley traces the history and origin of the peoples in each part of the world, and the effect such factors as climate and migration have had upon them.

MINERALS AND ROCKS IN COLOUR
by Prof: J.F. Kirkaldy

Professor Kirkaldy has written a condensed and masterly text of some 30,000 words which packs into this small format book all the essential information relating to mineral and rock species, details of localities where they may be found, their mode of occurrence and their economic uses.
267 photographs reproduced in superb colour are accurate and of exceptional quality.